07 NOV 09

23. MAR 10

DROITWICH

D0716342

Please return/renew this item by the last date shown

T
worcestershire
countycouncil
Libraries & Learning

70003

PA
GA

PASTA
GALORE

VALENTINA HARRIS

spruce

An Hachette UK Company

First published in Great Britain in 2009
by Spruce, a division of
Octopus Publishing Group Ltd
2–4 Heron Quays, London E14 4JP.
www.octopusbooks.co.uk

Copyright © Octopus Publishing Group Ltd,
2009

All rights reserved. No part of this work may be
reproduced or utilized in any form or by any
means, electronic or mechanical, including
photocopying, recording or by any information
storage and retrieval system without the prior
written permission of the publisher.

ISBN-13 978-1-84601-318-8

A CIP catalogue record of this book is available
from the British Library.

10 9 8 7 6 5 4 3 2 1

Printed and bound in China

Many thanks to the Barilla Group
(http://int.primopiatto.barilla.com) for kindly
supplying pasta to use when making the
recipes for the photographic shoot.

Photography: Ian Garlick
Food styling: Valentina Harris
Page layout: Balley Design Ltd

This book contains the opinions and ideas of
the author. It is intended to provide helpful and
informative material on the subjects addressed
in this book and is sold with the understanding
that the author and publisher are not engaged
in rendering any kind of personal professional
services in this book. The author and publisher
disclaim all responsibility for any liability, loss
or risk, personal or otherwise, that is incurred
as a consequence, directly or indirectly, of the
use and application of any of the contents of
this book.

The Department of Health advises that eggs
should not be consumed raw. This book contains
some dishes made with raw eggs. It is prudent
for more vulnerable people, such as pregnant
or nursing mothers, invalids, the elderly, babies
and young children, to avoid dishes made with
uncooked or lightly cooked eggs.
• All eggs used in the recipes, including making
pasta, should be large.
• Where fresh pasta is not stated, use dried.

Picture Credits
Shutterstock/Olga Semicheva p.10/Kmitu p.19.

CONTENTS

INTRODUCTION

Of all the wonderful dishes that Italy has given the world, a bowl of perfectly prepared pasta has to be the most special. Nothing seems to provoke as much passion and fervour in a real Italian in the kitchen as his or her favourite recipe.

★ CHOOSING AND USING PASTA ★

Pasta is such an incredibly versatile ingredient. It can be served in a soup, stuffed with a delicious filling, layered and baked, or tossed in a sauce. It can be combined also with cheese, fresh or cured meat, and any manner of vegetables, pulses, fish and seafood – even leftovers can be transformed into a tasty frittata.

The right combination of pasta shape and sauce is something that every Italian takes very seriously indeed. In general, if the choice is correct, there should be very little, if any, sauce left behind after serving. In general, any sauce can be used with dried pasta, but fresh pasta, being more delicate and rich, should be used with gentler-tasting, creamier sauces. The perfect illustration is

Puttanesca, which is far too strong and aggressive in flavour to be used with fresh pasta. Chunky sauces dress short pasta shapes, while smooth sauces mainly go with long pasta, but there are countless exceptions. In Italy, pasta is not normally served with any specific accompaniment – bread, salad or simply a glass of wine – whatever you feel like, if anything at all.

★ TYPES OF PASTA ★

There are over 650 different pasta shapes available and listed here are some of the most popular.

Bucatini – a thick, hollow, spaghetti-shaped pasta.

Cannolicchi – Short pasta tubes with wide grooves running around the outside.

Capelli d'angelo (angel hair) – Fine egg pasta cut into light golden strands.

Cellentani – Short, narrow pasta tubes shaped like a corkscrew.

Conchiglie – 'Seashells' in Italian and good for cupping sauces; giant-sized jumbo conchiglie can be filled.

Ditalini (little thimbles) – Short tubes traditionally added to minestrone or *pasta e fagioli*.

Farfalle (butterflies) – Pasta bows.

Fusilli – This twisting shape should really be called *Eliche* (propellors) because real **Eliche** are long, corkscrew spaghetti.

Lasagna sheets – Much-loved flat sheets of pasta.

Maccheroni – Straight-ended tubular pasta shapes; **Rigatoni** is a slightly bigger, wide-ribbed version.

Mafaldine – A long ribbon pasta with ruffles along the long edges that is about 1cm wide.

Maltagliati – thick, short pasta tubes with diagonally cut ends.

Orecchiette – Little ears from the south of Italy.

Pappardelle – Wide tagliatelle (below); **Reginette** are similar, with frilled edges that hold more sauce.

Penne – Smooth or ribbed tubes. There are several sub-versions such as **Pennette** (small penne) **Mezze Penne** (halved penne) and **Pennoni** (supersize penne).

Ruote or rotelle – Round, spoked wheels.

Spaghetti – The original classic remains the most popular shape. **Vermicelli** is a slightly thicker version; **Linguine** are long, thin ribbons, like flattened spaghetti; **Bavette** are wider and flatter than linguine.

Stelline – tiny star-shaped pasta often used in soups.

Tagliatelle – Flat pasta ribbons.

Taglierini, also known as tagliolini, is about 6mm wide and is a narrower ribbon pasta than tagliatelle.

Trenette – a long ribbon pasta about 7mm wide with a ripple edge on one side only.

Ziti – The original, factory-made pasta shape from the days when the only way of cutting pasta was in long tubes like hose pipes, which could then be cut to the right length.

THE ORIGINS OF PASTA

Since the turn of the last century, Italians have travelled far and wide, always accompanied by their favourite pasta, so it has become a much-loved international staple. Unlike many other Italian foods, pasta goes back hundreds, if not thousands of years.

★ THE FIRST PASTA ★

Venetian merchant and traveller Marco Polo is reputed to have introduced pasta after his journeys in China, but an Etruscan type made from lagane (spelt flour, and the origin of lasagna) was first recorded in the 1st century AD. It was not boiled, but oven-cooked. Later, the Romans baked and then cut lagane in strips, adding it to other ingredients boiled in liquid, and so created the first pasta with a dressing: *lagane et ciceris* (pasta with chickpeas).

It is well known that the Arab invasions of the 8th century influenced the cuisine of Sicily and much of southern Italy. The most accepted theory is that dried pasta first appeared in Sicily as *ittriya* – flour and water dough twisted around a stick, like curly spaghetti. Maccheroni derives from the Sicilian term for forcing the dough; early pasta making was a laborious, lengthy process. How exactly it was served is unknown, but many Sicilian recipes include Arab ingredients like raisins and cinnamon. It soon became a staple and its popularity subsequently spread to the mainland, where durum wheat grows prolifically.

TOMATO SAUCE AND PASTA

It was not until the mid 19th century that the first tomatoes were eaten. They were deemed poisonous, an idea that might have some foundation as they belong to the deadly nightshade (*belladonna*) family. Others believed them to be the apple from the Garden of Eden. It was not until 1839 that a pasta recipe with tomatoes was documented, following which they were accepted and increasingly popular as a sauce, especially in southern Italy.

By the 1300s dried pasta, with its nutritional qualities and long shelf life, was popular for sea voyages and therefore introduced around the globe in subsequent centuries, while new shapes and recipes evolved – there are now more than 650 types.

Pasta was not served at the tables of the aristocracy in Naples until after the fork was introduced towards the end of the 18th century, during King Ferdinand II's reign. Before, it was largely eaten with the fingers as a street food. Once use of the fork became widespread, it was served all over Italy and thereafter worldwide. US President Thomas Jefferson (1743–1826) first fell in love with pasta he sampled in Naples while serving as Ambassador to France. He promptly ordered crates of maccheroni and a pasta machine to be sent back to the USA. Legend has it that the popular song 'Yankee Doodle Dandy' – 'He stuck a feather in his cap and called it maccheroni' – refers to this episode.

★ PASTA MACHINES & MODERN TECHNOLOGY ★

At the beginning of the last century, basic industrial machines for pasta production were installed in small factories along the coastline of towns such as Castellammare di Stabia, near Naples. Sea breezes helped in the all-important drying process, but today modern technology allows standardization of production processes and factories can be found all over the country. It is estimated that Italians now eat over 27 kilograms of pasta per person per year, easily outstripping the Americans, who consume about 9 kilogrammes each.

DRIED VERSUS FRESH PASTA

There's a world of difference between fresh and dried durum wheat pasta, as well as subsections of dried egg pasta, wholewheat, dried soft wheat and pasta made from other grains for people who suffer a wheat intolerance, but still want to enjoy the occasional plate of pasta.

★ DRIED PASTA ★

Dried durum wheat pasta, such as classic spaghetti, has to be made under factory conditions because it requires a specific method of kneading, cutting and especially drying or it will fall apart during cooking. It is made with hard wheat flour mixed with water.

This type of pasta is eaten all over Italy and each region has its own specific shapes and formats. These go particularly well with the recipes belonging to those areas, and there are shapes not necessarily found outside the regions that are part of the culinary traditions. Having said that, the most popular shape of all remains spaghetti, closely followed by penne. Spaghetti is numbered according to the size of die used to cut it and some purists are very particular about which size of spaghetti is used in specific recipes.

★ WHOLEWHEAT PASTA ★

This pasta has a strong flavour of its own, which makes it hard to appreciate the quality of sauce used to dress the finished dish. Regular durum wheat pasta that is cooked al dente (firm to the bite) usually provides plenty of roughage. Conversely, if the pasta is overcooked, it will turn into a solid, glutinous mass that is much harder to digest.

It is important to respect the al dente rule because not only will the pasta dish taste so much better, it will also be far more beneficial from a digestive perspective. It is noticeable that the further south one travels in Italy, the more al dente the pasta served. In Naples, they sometimes serve spaghetti that is only just bendy. This is a little too extreme for most people, but for the Neapolitans it is perfectly normal and anything cooked for longer is considered overcooked.

★ SOUTHERN PASTA ★

Another type of pasta that should be mentioned is the very dense, often homemade shape, such as orecchiette, cavatelli or strascinapreti, from Italy's southernmost regions. These are made with soft wheat flour or hard wheat flour (or a combination of both) and then mixed with water and air-dried. They are very dense, which means they take a long time to cook until tender and once cooked, are quite spongy in texture. Typically, they are only really found in Puglia, Basilicata and Calabria.

★ FRESH PASTA ★

Mostly found in the north of Italy, fresh pasta made with eggs is known as pasta *all'uovo* or *la sfoglia*. It is said to have originated in Emilia Romagna, which also produces Parma ham, Mortadella and many other cured meats, as well as Balsamic vinegar. This region alone produces 60 per cent of food products eaten anywhere in Italy. Shapes such as tagliatelle, ravioli, tortellini, tortelloni, cannelloni and lasagna began here, while neighbouring regions have their own versions.

PASTA, ITALIAN-STYLE

With a hand-cranked machine, fresh egg pasta is relatively easy to make at home. Learning how to achieve the same effect by hand, with a rolling pin and plenty of elbow grease, is considerably harder and several attempts may be required before success can be reached.

★ A TRADITIONAL ART ★

Naturally, there is a vast difference between pasta lovingly made by hand and so-called 'fresh' pasta that one buys in a shop. Italians will tell you that the most important ingredients in fresh egg pasta – which are only really noticeable by their absence – are the love and gossip flying around the kitchen when the pasta was made; this is due to the fact that fresh pasta is only ever really made at home for special occasions such as weddings or christenings, when the family gets together en masse and there are enough people to help with the process. The rest of the time, most Italians enjoy fresh egg pasta in a restaurant, or they will be perfectly happy to eat best-quality dried durum wheat pasta with a good sauce on it. After all, the pasta is the vehicle that carries the sauce and while it would never do to waste good sauce on poor pasta, or to put a poor or inappropriate dressing on to special pasta, the important thing to remember is that for a truly memorable dish, the two must combine.

For many Italians, it is generally considered preferable to eat dried egg pasta (*pasta all'uovo*) that has been factory-made and then dried, rather than soft fresh pasta, which is made industrially rather than by hand. Because fresh pasta tends to be more delicate and sophisticated than the dried durum wheat variety, it does not suit all sauces. While almost any sauce may be used to dress hard wheat pasta, only certain sauces will

enhance and flatter the special qualities of fresh pasta. In this book, I have specified fresh pasta in the recipes where this will achieve the best result.

★ BASIC PASTA DOUGH ★

Blending flour, either soft wheat flour or a combination of hard wheat flour (durum wheat) and soft wheat flour, with eggs creates the basic pasta dough. Usually the proportion is 100g to 1 egg per person, although some variations exist (see also page 19). Fresh egg pasta quantities, when making pasta from scratch, are measured in eggs.

★ TEXTURE AND FINISH ★

Pasta cut with a plastic die is much smoother than with the more traditional bronze die that gives a visibly rougher finish. A rougher finish means sauce adheres to the surface more easily, but this is very much a question of personal taste and also depends on the sauce selected to dress the pasta. In any case, good pasta is absorbent and allows the sauce to actually permeate the shape itself. Wise cooks will save some of the boiling-hot water from draining their pasta to help distribute the sauce as they toss everything together, and this is especially useful when cooking for large numbers.

PASTA PERFECTION

To achieve the best possible results for a plate of perfectly dressed pasta – *pastasciutta*, to distinguish it from baked or stuffed pasta, pasta soups or pasta salads – listed here are my golden rules for cooking perfect pasta:

★ Pasta likes plenty of water to cook in when it is being boiled. The ratio is 5 litres water to 1 kilogram of pasta.

★ Make sure the water is properly salted before adding the pasta. The correct amount of salt is 7 grams per kilo.

★ Check the water is really boiling before you add the pasta to the saucepan.

★ Replace the lid on the saucepan once the pasta is completely immersed in the boiling water to return to the boil as fast as possible. When the water returns to the boil, remove the lid and continue boiling, stirring the pasta from time to time.

★ The only way to really tell if pasta is cooked the way you like it is to lift a little out of the saucepan with a slotted spoon and taste it. Once you are happy with the level of tenderness, drain and dress the pasta quickly, bearing in mind that it will continue to cook for as long as it is hot. Italians enjoy their pasta al dente (firm to the bite).

★ Remember that all fresh pasta cooks much more quickly and that the al dente rule doesn't really apply when dealing with fresh pasta or pasta soups.

★ Always serve your pasta piping hot on warmed plates or bowls.

★ And finally, never accompany a fishy pasta dish with grated cheese!

EQUIPMENT

The most important piece of equipment to have in your kitchen is a set of good knives that are kept sharp. A large, wide-bladed knife can be used for chopping and slicing, while a smaller one is perfect for paring, peeling and trimming.

★ KITCHEN BASICS ★

Strong, sharp kitchen scissors make it so much easier to cut meat or fish into strips, or to finely snip herbs or vegetables. Another useful item is the mezzaluna, a crescent-shaped blade with a handle at each end, used to finely chop garlic, herbs and other ingredients.

A food processor or blenders save time and makes all kinds of procedures possible. Soup or a smooth sauce can be whizzed up in minutes. You can also chop, shred and slice more finely than ever before.

Also essential is a large saucepan and metal colander that will hold large quantities of pasta comfortably and can be used to clean and prepare vegetables, while doubling up as a steamer with a tight-fitting lid.

Finally, look for a saucepan with a heavy base so the heat is distributed evenly when making soups and sauces. A heavy-based frying pan is also important, while a good-quality non-stick pan saves time.

★ PASTA MACHINES ★

These exist as simple, old-fashioned hand-cranked machines, or as much more complicated electrical versions. The hand-cranked model is favoured by most as long as it is made in Italy and is of a good old-fashioned family firm such as Imperia or Augusta. These are great fun to use, almost impossible to break and give smooth, even, silky pasta.

★ CUTTING SHAPES & ELECTRIC MACHINES ★

The basic machine cuts pasta into tagliatelle or tagliolini/spaghetti, but other units can be added on to make pappardelle and other long ribbon shapes.

Lots more shapes, including short penne or maccheroni, can be achieved in an electric model. In the case of these machines, many of which also make dough, just follow the accompanying instructions. Despite developments, nothing beats an extra-long, heavy rolling pin, which easily stretches and flattens the sheet of dough ready for cooking.

IMPORTANT

Never wash your pasta machine, or allow moisture to get inside. It won't dry, will definitely rust and thereafter become useless. After use, simply brush clean (you should only need to remove excess flour) and replace in the box until the next time you plan to use it. Store in a dry place.

★ EXTRA ATTACHMENTS ★

It is possible to add attachments to the basic machine, such as a ravioli-making tray, but it is questionable whether these are really so efficient as using a tabletop, cutter or sharp knife. Ravioli trays (a little like ice-cube trays) are also available to buy separately. The dough is laid on the base, filling added and then the second sheet of pasta goes on top. A mini rolling pin cuts the dough exactly where it is supposed to and seals in the filling. Afterwards, it is simply a matter of tipping out the uniform, sealed ravioli.

HOW TO MAKE FRESH PASTA

To explain how to make fresh pasta (*la sfoglia*) in writing is hard to do. In addition to these instructions, I recommend that you attend a pasta-making class with an expert so that you can see for yourself what happens during this magical process! Bear in mind that no two batches of flour are identical, and that no two eggs are ever quite the same, so if you do end up having to add more egg or more flour to your mixture, this is not an indication of failure on your part.

★ BASIC PASTA DOUGH ★

INGREDIENTS (PER PERSON)

100g plain white pasta flour, 00, or half plain white flour and half semola or fine semolina (semola is made from hard Durum wheat whereas semolina is made from softer types of wheat); 1 large egg and extra flour for rolling out.

1. To make pasta, pile all the flour onto a work surface and plunge your fist into the centre to make a hollow. Break the eggs into a bowl and whisk together briefly to combine and then pour into the hollow.

2. Using your fingertips, begin to roughly knead the flour, then use whole hands to knead everything together. It's not like making pastry, so this is not the moment for a delicate approach! On the other hand, if you are too heavy-handed, you will cause the dough to dry out too much and it will never roll out smoothly.

3. Knead the flour and eggs together until you have a really smooth, pliable ball of dough. Rest under a clean cloth for about 20 minutes to relax the gluten and make the dough more manageable.

4. Now comes the hard part: on a floured surface, roll the dough out as thinly as possible with a strong long rolling pin. Continue rolling over and over again until your dough is really elastic, smooth and shiny.

5. You can use a pasta machine instead of the traditional rolling pin. As before, knead together the eggs and flour into a rough textured ball of dough.

6. Wrap and rest the dough for 20 minutes, then unwrap and cover with a slightly damp cloth to prevent it drying out. Break off a piece about the size of a small fist.

7. Flatten this piece out with your hands and push through the widest setting on your pasta machine, turning the handle.

8. Fold in half and repeat 3 or 4 times, or until the pasta snaps as it moves between the rollers, having become taut and thus created an air pocket. Once this has happened, move the machine down to the next setting. Repeat twice. Continue, changing the setting after 2 complete windings on each number, down to the last or penultimate setting on the machine, depending on how fine you want the pasta to be. Lay the sheets of pasta out carefully on a floured surface.

9. Now take another lump of dough the size of a small fist and begin again. Repeat until all the dough has been used up. Make sure all the sheets of pasta are of the same thickness (i.e. that the final process was through the same setting on the machine each time), or they will cook unevenly.

10. Once cut, use the pasta immediately or let it dry out further. Dried-out fresh egg pasta can be kept in a sealed jar in a dry place for up to 1 month. Alternatively, open-freeze on trays, then bag up and label with the date; it will keep for up to 3 months, once frozen.

★ FILLED PASTA SHAPES ★

Fresh egg pasta is also used to make the many different filled pasta shapes to be found in the central and northern regions of Italy. When making filled pasta by hand, remember not to let the pasta dough dry out before trying to fill it, or the pasta will stop sticking altogether, causing the filling to fall out during the cooking process. Fillings can be made with a variety of different ingredients, but the ratio of pasta to filling can be surprising for novice cooks, as there is really very little filling compared to the amount of pasta used. This is because the pasta needs to be really finely rolled out and the filling must be intense in flavour for the dish to be balanced and also to ensure that the filled pasta won't burst while cooking.

PASTA TIP – WORKING WITH DOUGH

To help ensure you achieve the best results when making your own fresh pasta, here are a couple of helpful tips:

★ The dough cools down considerably as you work it, and you will notice it dropping in temperature as you follow the steps. When it is ready, the sheet of dough will feel like a brand new, wrung-out damp chamois – shiny, cool, elastic sheet – but it must not be too brittle.

★ If using a food processor to knead the dough, whizz for about 45 seconds at a time, checking the texture of the dough between each turn.

★ To keep the pasta moist, cover the dough with a slightly damp cloth when you are not working with it.

★ Keep an eye on the sheets of pasta you have rolled out. Place on a floured surface to dry, but remember they will not be easy to cut if they are too dry.

★ FILLING & SHAPING TORTELLONI ★

TO MAKE SQUARES

Begin to work with 1 strip of pasta at a time. Cut into equal squares, the small the better – though too small will mean you can't make the tortelloni at all! Cut out just a couple of squares of different sizes to begin with to see what size works best for you. Drop $1/4$ teaspoon filling in the centre of each square. Fold in half to make a triangle and seal the edges with your fingertips. If the pasta begins to dry out, dab the edges with a little cold water to moisten and help seal. Wind around the tip of your index finger, pressing the two outer ends of the triangle together firmly. Push off the end of your finger. Using both your hands, fold the ring outwards so that it looks like a perfect belly button!

PASTA TIP – WHEN FILLING PASTA

While making filled pasta, don't let the dough dry out: use it as soon as it is ready – the moist pasta will be easier to shape, twist and seal. You can cut your flat or unfilled pasta into the desired shape as soon as it is dry enough to roll up without sticking to itself. To test, squash between finger and thumb and see if you leave a dent.

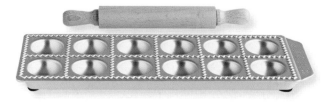

TO MAKE CIRCLES

Cut the fine dough into circles with a 4cm diameter biscuit cutter and put $1/4$ teaspoon filling in the centre. Fold in half and hold between your middle and index finger. Wrap the two extremities around the tip of your index finger. Push the filled pasta pocket off your finger and turn it half inside out so that it looks like a little belly button. Press the ends together and proceed to the next one.

MEAT

MACCHERONI WITH MORTADELLA

This is a really quick and simple, very tasty pasta dish, which requires no cooking. Mortadella, sometimes called Bologna, is a much-underrated cured meat from the region of Emilia Romagna in Italy.

SERVES 4

400g maccheroni
4 tablespoons unsalted butter
100g chopped Mortadella
80g grated Gruyère cheese
Sea salt and freshly ground
    black pepper

1. Bring a large saucepan of salted water to a rolling boil, then add the pasta and cook until al dente (firm to the bite) according to the package directions.

2. Meanwhile, place the butter, Mortadella and Gruyère in a large shallow bowl and mix together lightly to combine.

3. Drain and pour the pasta over the mixture in the bowl. Toss together quickly. Finish off with a little sea salt and freshly ground black pepper just before serving.

AGNOLOTTI PIEDMONTESE-STYLE

This is a long and labour-intensive dish but the end results are truly spectacular – it really is worth the effort! Agnolotti are a Piedmontese version of ravioli.

SERVES 8

300g beef rump, cubed
1 carrot, chopped
1 celery stick, chopped
3 cloves, lightly crushed
1 garlic clove, peeled and crushed
5 peppercorns
3 tablespoons olive oil
Enough red wine to cover
12 thinly sliced pancetta rashers
500g spinach, thoroughly rinsed and
    picked over
300ml milk
Pasta (see page 28)
50g rice
5 eggs, beaten
5 tablespoons freshly grated
    Parmesan cheese, plus extra
    to serve
A large pinch of nutmeg.
Sea salt and freshly ground black
    pepper

1. Place the meat in a large bowl with the carrot, celery, cloves, garlic, peppercorns and oil. Cover with red wine and leave to stand overnight.

2. The next day, line a large pan with the pancetta and cover with the contents of the bowl. Cook slowly over a very low heat for about 4 hours.

3. In a pan, cook the spinach with the water clinging to the leaves until wilted, 3–4 minutes. Cool, drain and squeeze out all the excess water.

4. In a saucepan, bring the milk to the boil. Add the rice and simmer until tender, about 15 minutes. Drain and discard any remaining milk.

5. To make the pasta dough, combine the flour and semolina, and then pile onto a work surface. Make a well in the centre with your fist. Break the eggs and egg yolk into a bowl, then beat together with a fork.

6. Pour the eggs into the hollow and knead roughly with your hands into the flour. Continue kneading until you have a really smooth, pliable ball of dough. Cover with a cloth and leave to rest for 20 minutes.

7. Mince the cooked meat with the rice and spinach, then add the eggs and grated Parmesan cheese and mix well. Season generously with salt, pepper and nutmeg and then mix together very thoroughly.

PASTA

750g plain white pasta flour, 00,
  plus extra for rolling out
55g fine semolina
8 eggs and 1 egg yolk

DRESSING

150g unsalted butter, melted
  (keep hot)
1 rosemary sprig
1 sage sprig

8. On a floured surface, roll out the pasta as thinly as possible into 2 equal sheets about the width of a hand (a machine will automatically size them). Spacing them well apart (about two fingers between each mound), place the filling along 1 sheet of pasta.

9. Cover with the second sheet of pasta, then cut around the filling with a pastry wheel or serrated cookie or pasta cutter to form circles about 6cm in diameter.

10. Bring a large pan of salted water to the boil and drop the agnolotti into the water in batches, removing with a slotted spoon as soon as they float to the surface. Transfer to a heatproof serving dish.

11. Cover the pasta with the hot melted butter, add the rosemary and sage and infuse over a pan of simmering water for about 1 hour. Serve with extra Parmesan, nutmeg and ground black pepper.

PASTA TIMBALES WITH PEPPERS & MINI MEATBALLS

These very pretty individual rounds are easy enough to make but look impressive and taste wonderful. Vary the flavour by adding little fish balls instead of meat into the meatball filling. The meatballs may also be served on their own as canapés.

MAKES 4 TIMBALES

4 large red peppers
200g fresh penne
8 tablespoons olive oil
1 onion, peeled and chopped
400g chopped tomatoes
1 handful of basil leaves
200g mozzarella cheese, cubed
Parmesan cheese, to taste
10 Lemon Meatballs (see page 32)
Wild rocket, lightly dressed in lemon
   juice and extra virgin olive oil,
   to serve
Sea salt and freshly ground pepper

1. Preheat the oven to 180°C/350°F/Gas Mark 4. Lay the peppers on a baking sheet and roast until softened. Remove the skins, deseed and cut into large slices. Use to line 4 oiled Dariole moulds or ramekin dishes, leaving some pepper slightly overhanging to fold over in Step 5.

2. Bring a saucepan of salted water to a rolling boil. Add the pasta and cook until al dente (firm to the bite) according to the package directions. Drain and lightly coat in 2 tablespoons olive oil.

3. Meanwhile, heat 2 tablespoons olive oil in a frying pan and fry the onion until softened. Add the tomatoes and mix together. Simmer for 10 minutes and then stir in the basil and seasoning.

4. Gently stir the sauce and pasta together to combine. Add the mozzarella, Parmesan to taste and the cooked meatballs.

LEMON MEATBALLS

400g minced veal, beef, turkey
   or chicken
100g fresh breadcrumbs
100g grated Parmesan or Grana
   Padano cheese
3 large eggs
3 tablespoons chopped flat leaf
   parsley
1/2 wine glass of cold water
Grated zest of 1 lemon and juice
   of 1/2 lemon
5 tablespoons fine dry breadcrumbs
Sunflower seed oil, for deep-frying
Sea salt and freshly ground
   black pepper

5. Pack the filling into the prepared moulds or ramekins. Fold the peppers back over the top to enclose. Bake for about 10 minutes until slightly browned and then remove from the oven.

6. Leave to rest for 5 minutes to firm up and then turn out onto warmed plates. Surround with dressed rocket leaves and serve.

LEMON MEATBALLS

1. In a bowl, mix together thoroughly the meat, breadcrumbs, cheese, 1 egg, seasoning and parsley, then gradually blend in the water. Finally, stir in the lemon zest and juice.

2. Mix with your hands for a few minutes, then shape the mixture into small, cherry-sized balls.

3. Beat the remaining 2 eggs, then roll the meatballs in the egg and then the breadcrumbs.

4. Heat the sunflower oil until a cube of bread dropped onto the surface sizzles instantly. Deep-fry the meatballs for a few minutes until crisp and brown, turning frequently. Drain on kitchen paper.

CLASSIC RAGÙ ALLA BOLOGNESE

This very old-fashioned sauce is traditionally used to dress tagliatelle and yields enough to dress 400g pasta. The important thing is to keep the meat looking like chopped meat rather than mince.

SERVES 4

100g pork loin, boned
100g beef steak, boned
100g prosciutto crudo
100g unsalted butter
1 carrot, finely chopped
1 celery stick, finely chopped
1 onion, peeled and finely chopped
50g pancetta or bacon (rind
  removed), finely chopped
1 heaped tablespoon tomato purée
  diluted in 300ml hot water
225ml hot stock or water
100g chicken livers, washed, trimmed
  and finely chopped
6 tablespoons double or single cream
1 small truffle, cleaned and thinly
  sliced (optional)
Sea salt and freshly ground
  black pepper

1. With a heavy knife, chop the meats together finely.

2. In a frying pan, melt half the butter and fry the vegetables and pancetta or bacon for 5–6 minutes, stirring.

3. Stir in the chopped meat and fry until sealed all over. Add the diluted tomato purée and season with salt and pepper. Stir well, cover and leave to simmer very slowly for about 2 hours until tender, stirring frequently. Do not let the mixture dry out – keep adding hot stock or water.

4. Add the chicken livers and simmer for 5 minutes, then stir in the cream, remaining butter and truffle, if using.

5. Serve at once or leave to stand for an hour or overnight, if possible. The sauce will improve in flavour if you leave it to stand and then reheat slowly for 20 minutes, stirring occasionally.

LASAGNA

This rich and creamy dish remains one of the most popular of all pasta dishes ever created. Here is how to make it with fresh pasta that you have made yourself, although to save time you could use bought fresh pasta or even 500g dried oven-ready lasagna.

SERVES 6

2 tablespoons olive oil
1 large onion, peeled and finely
   chopped
1 large carrot, finely chopped
1 large celery stick, finely chopped
400g lean minced beef or veal
1 glass of dry red wine
500ml passata (sieved tomatoes)
1 handful of dried porcini mushrooms
   (soak in warm water for at least
   1 hour)
3 tablespoons freshly grated
   Parmesan cheese
120g mozzarella, cubed
Sea salt and freshly ground
   black pepper
PASTA
500g plain white pasta flour, 00, plus
   extra for rolling out
6 large eggs

1. First, make the fresh pasta (see pages 19–20). Roll out on a floured surface as thinly as possible and then cut into rectangles about the same size as your palm.

2. Bring a pan of salted water to a rolling boil, then cook the lasagna in batches, 3 sheets at a time. As soon as the sheets rise to the surface, remove with a slotted spoon and lay flat in a wide bowl or tray of cold water to prevent them from sticking together.

3. To start off the sauce, heat the olive oil in a frying pan and gently fry together the onion, carrot and celery for about 10 minutes to soften. Add the minced meat and fry until well browned, turning.

4. Stir in the red wine and quickly boil for 2 minutes, then stir in the tomatoes. Return to the boil and then reduce the heat to a low simmer. Leave to cook slowly, stirring frequently, for about $1\frac{1}{2}$ hours, then drain and coarsely chop the mushrooms, reserving the soaking liquid. Stir into the sauce.

5. Strain the soaking liquid through a double layer of kitchen paper or muslin, then add to the sauce. Season, stir and simmer for a further hour.

BÉCHAMEL SAUCE

75g unsalted butter

5 level tablespoons plain white pasta
flour, 00

750ml milk

A pinch of grated nutmeg

Sea salt

6. Prepare the Béchamel sauce by melting the butter in a saucepan. Add the flour and mix together to form a roux. Pour in the milk and whisk to prevent lumps forming. Add salt and nutmeg to taste. Simmer gently (about 15 minutes) stirring constantly, until the sauce is thick enough to coat the back of a spoon.

7. Remove the pan from the heat and sprinkle the surface with a little cold water to prevent a skin forming. Set aside until needed.

8. Preheat the oven to 200°C/400°F/Gas Mark 6. To assemble the lasagna, cover the base of a large rectangular ovenproof dish (about 20cm square) with a layer of pasta, then a layer of meat sauce, followed by a thin layer of Parmesan, a sprinkling of mozzarella and a layer of Béchamel sauce.

9. Repeat until you have used up all the ingredients, finishing with a layer of Béchamel and a final dusting of Parmesan. Leave to stand for about 10 minutes, then bake for 30 minutes until golden and bubbling.

10. Remove from the oven and leave to stand for at least 5 minutes to firm up before dividing into squares to serve.

MACCHERONI WITH PROSCIUTTO

This is a very quick and simple pasta dish, really tasty and satisfying. Use bacon instead of the prosciutto, if you prefer.

SERVES 4

4 tablespoons unsalted butter
3 sage leaves
1 rosemary sprig
150g chopped prosciutto crudo
400g maccheroni
3 tablespoons freshly grated Grana
   Padano cheese, plus extra to serve
Sea salt and freshly ground
   black pepper

1. First, warm the butter in a small pan with the sage and rosemary. As soon as it starts to sizzle, add the prosciutto crudo and some freshly ground black pepper.

2. Bring a large saucepan of salted water to a rolling boil. Add the pasta and stir once. Cook according to the package directions until al dente (firm to the bite). Drain, reserving a little of the cooking water, and stir into the same pan with the ham and herbs.

3. Mix together, adding the Grana Padano and a little of the pasta cooking water.

4. Remove and discard the herbs. Season well and transfer the pasta to a warmed bowl or individual pasta bowls to serve. Offer extra cheese separately at the table.

BUCATINI ALL'AMATRICIANA

Amatrice, where this dish comes from, is a small town near Rome that is famous for its fantastic pork products. This is a real classic – rich and piquant, flavoured with delicious smoked pancetta.

SERVES 4

3 tablespoons extra virgin
  olive oil
300g smoked pancetta, cubed
1 onion, peeled and finely chopped
3 garlic cloves, peeled and chopped
½–2 dried red chilli peppers
  (according to preference), deseeded
  and finely chopped
600g canned tomatoes, drained and
  coarsely chopped
400g bucatini (or other dried durum
  wheat pasta with a chunky shape)
75g Pecorino or Parmesan cheese,
  grated, to serve
Sea salt and freshly ground black
  pepper

1. Heat the oil in a pan and fry the pancetta until the fat is transparent and runs freely.

2. Add the onion, garlic and chilli peppers and gently fry until the onion is soft and translucent.

3. Stir in the tomatoes and season, then cover and simmer for 20 minutes, stirring frequently. When the sauce is thick and glossy, bring a large saucepan of salted water to a rolling boil and cook the pasta until al dente (firm to the bite) according to the package directions.

4. Drain the pasta thoroughly, return to the saucepan and pour in the sauce. Mix together thoroughly to combine. Arrange on a warmed serving dish and serve with the cheese offered separately.

PASTA AL FORNO

This is a very simple and easy baked pasta dish that I remember very fondly from my childhoood in Tuscany. Really, I prefer to use penne when I make this, as it fits the memory much better, but conchiglie works, too.

SERVES 4

400g penne or conchiglie, or
   another short pasta
500ml Béchamel sauce
   (see pages 34–5)
6 tablespoons freshly grated
   Parmesan cheese
200g best baked ham, chopped
3 tablespoons unsalted butter
Sea salt and freshly ground
   black pepper

1. Bring a saucepan of salted water to a rolling boil and cook the pasta according to the package directions until al dente (firm to the bite).

2. Meanwhile, heat through the sauce and melt three-quarters of the cheese into it.

3. Drain the pasta and return to the saucepan. Add three-quarters of the sauce and the chopped ham. Season and mix together to combine.

4. Preheat the oven to 200°C/400°F/Gas Mark 6. Meanwhile, grease a large ovenproof dish with half the butter. Tip in the dressed pasta and arrange carefully.

5. Pour over the remaining sauce and dot with the rest of the butter. Sprinkle with the remaining cheese. Bake for about 15 minutes until golden and bubbling. Remove, leave to rest for 5 minutes and then serve.

PASTA TIP
You can of course add other ingredients to this dish, such as chopped grilled bacon, cooked peas, mushrooms, cauliflower florets or blue cheese, for a much stronger flavour.

MAFALDINE ALLA ROMANA

Linguine, bavette or tagliatelle will also work with this sauce if mafaldine (narrow fettucine) are unavailable. You can use canned cherry tomatoes instead of fresh if you prefer.

SERVES 4

2 tablespoons dried porcini
   mushrooms
300g cherry tomatoes
3 tablespoons extra virgin olive oil
1 onion, peeled and finely chopped
3 tablespoons cubed smoked
   pancetta
300g mafaldine
3 tablespoons freshly grated Grana
   Padano cheese
2 tablespoons unsalted butter
1 handful of fresh flat leaf parsley,
   finely chopped, to garnish
Sea salt and freshly ground
   black pepper

1. First, soak the mushrooms for at least 20 minutes in hand-hot water until softened. Meanwhile, blanch, peel and deseed the cherry tomatoes, then finely chop.

2. In a large frying pan, warm the oil and then fry the onion and pancetta until the pancetta is crisp and the onion is golden brown.

3. Drain and chop the mushrooms, discarding the soaking water, and then add to the pancetta and onions. Mix together and stir in the tomatoes. Season with salt and pepper and simmer for 15 minutes.

4. Bring a large saucepan of salted water to a rolling bowl, then add the mafaldine and stir once. Boil until al dente (firm to the bite) according to the package directions and then drain.

5. Return the pasta to the pan with the sauce and mix together over a low heat for about 5 minutes, adding the grated cheese and butter.

6. Transfer to a warmed serving dish or individual warmed pasta bowls to serve at once, sprinkled with chopped parsley.

PAPPARDELLE WITH HARE

SERVES 4–6

500ml dry red wine
1 large onion, peeled and quartered
1 celery stick, quartered
5–6 peppercorns
A pinch of dried thyme
2 bay leaves
1.5kg hare, jointed into 8 sections
5 tablespoons olive oil
8 streaky bacon or pancetta rashers,
    chopped
A large pinch of freshly grated
    nutmeg
250ml beef or game stock
4 tablespoons unsalted butter
Sea salt and freshly ground
    black pepper
PASTA
250g plain white pasta flour, 00,
    plus extra for rolling out
3 eggs

1. Put the wine, onion, celery, peppercorns, thyme and bay leaves in a large bowl. Place the hare in the marinade, submerge thoroughly and then cover with clingfilm. Leave to stand in a cool place for about 12 hours.

2. Drain the hare joints, straining the marinade into a second bowl.

3. Put the oil and bacon or pancetta in a large, heavy-based saucepan and fry together gently until all the fat from the bacon runs.

4. Lay the hare joints in the saucepan and brown all over. Season to taste with nutmeg, salt and pepper. Cover and simmer gently for 1½ hours, adding the marinade and stock alternately every 10–15 minutes so that the meat stays moist throughout the cooking process. When the meat is very tender, remove the saucepan from the direct heat and keep warm until required.

5. Use the flour and eggs to make the fresh pasta (see pages 19–20). Slice into strips about the width of a man's thumb and of a length you can comfortably cook in your pasta saucepan.

6. Heat the hare until bubbling hot and meanwhile, bring a large saucepan of salted water to a rolling boil.

7. Remove the hare joints from the sauce, set aside and keep warm. Toss the pasta in the boiling water and stir (it should need about 3 minutes). Drain and return to the same saucepan.

8. Pour the sauce from the hare over the pasta and toss thoroughly. Add the butter and toss once more. Divide the pasta between 8 warmed plates and top each one with a joint of hare. Serve at once.

PASTA WITH PANCETTA & MUSHROOMS

SERVES 4

6 tablespoons cubed pancetta or chopped bacon
2 tablespoons unsalted butter
200g fresh mushrooms, wiped clean and thinly sliced
1 garlic clove, peeled and finely chopped
3 tablespoons double cream
400g maccheroni or other chunky pasta shape
3 tablespoons freshly grated Parmesan cheese
1 tablespoon finely chopped fresh flat leaf parsley, to garnish
Sea salt and freshly ground black pepper

1. Bring a large saucepan of salted water to a rolling boil. Meanwhile, fry the pancetta or bacon pieces in a non-stick frying pan until brown and crisp.

2. In a separate frying pan that is wide enough to hold all the mushrooms, melt the butter and fry the mushrooms and garlic together until the mushrooms are soft and well dried out. Stir in a little salt, the double cream and black pepper; keep warm.

3. Meanwhile, boil the pasta in the salted water until al dente (firm to the bite) according to the package directions. Drain thoroughly and return to the same saucepan.

4. Pour over the pancetta, mushroom and cream sauce. Toss together thoroughly and then add half the Parmesan. Toss once more.

5. Transfer the pasta and sauce to a warm platter or individual plates. Sprinkle with the remaining Parmesan and parsley.

MACCHERONI WITH PORK RAGÙ

This is a satisfying pasta dish with a lovely cheesy topping, dressed with a fragrant pork ragù. It's the perfect winter supper dish.

SERVES 4

3 tablespoons extra virgin olive oil
1 garlic clove, peeled and crushed
1 onion, peeled and finely chopped
200g coarsely minced pork
1 bay leaf
300ml pork or chicken stock
300g canned tomatoes, drained and chopped
350g maccheroni
1 tablespoon finely chopped rosemary
4 tablespoons unsalted butter
3 tablespoons dried breadcrumbs
4 tablespoons freshly grated Parmesan cheese
Sea salt and freshly ground black pepper

1. Preheat the oven to 220°C/425°F/Gas Mark 7. Meanwhile, heat the oil in a large frying pan and fry the garlic until golden. Discard the garlic, add the onion and fry until softened.

2. Transfer the meat to the pan and brown carefully. Add the bay leaf and seasoning with the hot stock and canned tomatoes. Stir, cover and simmer gently for about 50 minutes until the sauce is glossy and thick.

3. While the sauce is cooking, bring a large saucepan of salted water to a rolling boil. Add the pasta and cook according to the package directions until al dente (firm to the bite). Drain and return to the saucepan in which it was cooked.

4. Add the rosemary leaves and sauce to the saucepan and mix together thoroughly. Butter an ovenproof dish (about 20cm square), coat lightly with breadcrumbs and then transfer the dressed pasta. Sprinkle the top generously with cheese and dot with the remaining butter.

5. Bake in the oven for about 10 minutes until golden on top before serving straight from the dish.

MACCHERONI WITH MEATBALLS

Although traditionally one would serve this dish with spaghetti instead of maccheroni, somehow I feel that the short pasta shape works better in this instance.

SERVES 6

120ml olive oil
1 onion, peeled and chopped
500g minced pork and veal, mixed together
2 eggs, beaten
2½ tablespoons finely chopped flat leaf parsley
1 garlic clove, peeled and finely chopped
5–6 tablespoons fine dry breadcrumbs
750ml passata (sieved tomatoes)
1 handful of mixed herbs (sage, thyme, parsley and rosemary), finely chopped
500g large maccheroni
Rosemary sprigs, to garnish
Sea salt and freshly ground black pepper

1. Heat about 8 tablespoons of the oil in a large frying pan and fry the onion until softened. Remove from the heat and set aside until needed.

2. In a mixing bowl, blend the minced meat with the eggs, seasoning, parsley, garlic and 2–3 tablespoons breadcrumbs. Shape into balls about the size of large olives and roll in the remaining breadcrumbs.

3. Reheat the onion and oil and fry the meatballs until browned. Stir in the passata and chopped mixed herbs. Simmer together for about 1 hour, stirring frequently and adding a little water, if necessary.

4. Meanwhile, bring a large saucepan of salted water to a rolling boil. Cook the pasta in the boiling water according to the package directions until al dente (firm to the bite). Drain and return to the saucepan.

5. Pour over the sauce and meatballs. Toss together gently to avoid breaking up the meatballs. Transfer to a warmed serving dish or individual bowls and serve at once, garnished with rosemary sprigs.

TORTIGLIONI WITH LAMB

This wonderfully tasty lamb ragù is perfect served over pasta with a light dusting of pungent pecorino cheese to just cut the sweetness of the meat. Tortiglioni are slightly skewed maccheroni.

SERVES 4

4 tablespoons extra virgin olive oil

1 garlic clove, peeled and crushed lightly

1 bay leaf

1 rosemary sprig

1kg cubed lean lamb

1 dried red chilli pepper, chopped

1 glass of dry white wine

500g canned tomatoes, drained and chopped

2 red peppers, deseeded and diced

150ml lamb or beef stock

400g tortiglioni

Freshly grated mature pecorino cheese, to serve

Sea salt and freshly ground black pepper

1. Heat the oil in a large saucepan and fry the garlic, bay leaf and rosemary until the garlic is pungent and browned. Discard the garlic.

2. Add the meat to the pan and carefully brown all over. Stir in the chilli and season with salt and pepper.

3. Pour in half the wine and reduce the alcohol for a minute or so, then add the tomatoes and peppers. Stir and leave to simmer for 20 minutes.

4. Stir in the remaining wine and the stock. Continue to simmer until the meat begins to fall apart, at least an hour.

5. Meanwhile, bring a large saucepan of salted water to a rolling boil. Add the pasta and cook according to the package directions until al dente (firm to the bite). Drain and return to the same saucepan.

6. Add the sauce and mix together thoroughly. Transfer to a warmed serving dish or individual pasta bowls. Sprinkle generously with freshly grated pecorino and serve at once.

PASTA WITH SAUSAGE & CABBAGE

This is a deliciously wintry, warming pasta dish with lots of lovely flavours and textures. For a bit of crunch, add a handful of toasted pine kernels.

SERVES 4

4 tablespoons unsalted butter

1 large onion, peeled and thinly sliced

250g crumbled skinned Italian sausage (salsiccie di maiale or Lucanica)

1 small glass of dry white wine

250g shredded Savoy cabbage

150ml pork, chicken or vegetable stock

400g penne or other short pasta

A pinch of freshly grated nutmeg

8 tablespoons single or double cream

4 tablespoons freshly grated Parmesan cheese, to serve

Sea salt and freshly ground black pepper

1. Heat half the butter in a large saucepan and gently fry the onion until golden. Add the sausage and continue to cook until browned.

2. Pour in the white wine, then reduce for a minute or so before mixing in the cabbage. Cook until softened.

3. Bring a large saucepan of salted water to a rolling boil. If necessary, use a little of the water and the stock to dampen the cabbage as it cooks with the sausage and onion. Add the pasta to the saucepan of water and cook until al dente (firm to the bite) according to the package directions.

4. Meanwhile, once the cabbage has softened, add the nutmeg and stir in the cream, then season with salt and pepper. Remove from the heat and keep warm while the pasta continues cooking.

5. Drain the pasta, return to the saucepan in which it was cooked and add the sauce and remaining butter. Mix together thoroughly and then transfer to a warmed serving dish or individual pasta bowls. Sprinkle with freshly grated Parmesan and serve at once.

PENNETTE WITH SALAMI

Pennette are small penne that are neat, short and narrow and they are the best shape for this dish. If they can't be found, use regular penne instead.

SERVES 4

2 tablespoons unsalted butter
100g soft Italian salami, such as salami Milano or salami Toscano, peeled and chopped
½ glass of dry white wine
1 tablespoon concentrated tomato purée
400g pennette
4 tablespoons freshly grated Parmesan cheese, to serve
Sea salt and freshly ground black pepper

1. Bring a large saucepan of salted water to a rolling boil. Meanwhile, heat the butter in a frying pan and fry the salami until browned, then add the wine and tomato purée. Season, stir and simmer gently for about 5 minutes until the sauce begins to look glossy.

2. Cook the pasta in the boiling water according to the package directions until al dente (firm to the bite). Drain and return to the same saucepan. Add the sauce and mix together thoroughly to ensure the sauce is evenly distributed through the pasta.

3. Transfer to a warmed serving dish or individual pasta bowls and sprinkle with Parmesan just before serving.

RUOTE WITH PEA & SAUSAGE SAUCE

The spokes of the wheels in this pasta shape catch the peas and crumbs of sausage perfectly so that you get some with the pasta in every forkful.

SERVES 4

4 tablespoons olive oil
1 large onion, peeled and finely
    chopped
300g peas, frozen or freshly podded
4 large fresh Italian sausages, such
    as salsiccia di maiale, peeled
    and crumbled
5 tablespoons double cream
400g ruote (pasta wheels)
2–3 tablespoons freshly grated
    Parmesan cheese, to serve
Sea salt and freshly ground
    black pepper

1. Heat the oil in a large saucepan and fry the onion until softened, then add the peas and a little water. Simmer gently until the peas have softened, adding extra water if necessary, to prevent the pan from drying out.

2. Add the sausage meat to the peas. Cook together, stirring occasionally, until the sausages have browned well and the peas are soft.

3. Meanwhile, bring a large saucepan of salted water to a rolling boil and add the pasta. Stir the cream into the peas and sausage and keep the sauce warm.

4. Cook the pasta according to the package directions until al dente (firm to the bite). Drain and return to the saucepan.

5. Tip in the sausage and pea sauce and mix together thoroughly. Transfer to a warmed serving dish or pasta bowls and serve sprinkled with grated Parmesan.

MACCHERONI WITH SAUSAGE & ARTICHOKES

The ideal shaped pasta for this dish is called ditali, which means thimbles.
They are wide, short maccheroni that catch this sauce perfectly.

SERVES 4

350g short maccheroni
3 tablespoons extra virgin olive oil
250g peeled and crumbled Italian
    sausage
1 garlic clove, peeled and lightly
    crushed
10 artichoke hearts preserved in olive
    oil, drained and coarsely chopped
1 small handful of flat leaf parsley,
    chopped
Freshly grated Parmesan cheese,
    to serve
Sea salt and freshly ground
    black pepper

1. Bring a large saucepan of salted water to a rolling boil, then add the pasta and cook according to the package directions until al dente (firm to the bite).

2. Meanwhile, heat the olive oil in a large saucepan and fry the sausage and garlic until the sausage is well browned. Stir in the artichoke hearts, parsley and seasoning. Cook together for 1–2 minutes and keep warm.

3. Drain the pasta and return to the saucepan in which it was cooked. Tip in the sauce and mix together thoroughly.

4. Transfer to a warmed serving bowl or individual bowls and serve with the Parmesan offered separately.

TAJARIN WITH CHICKEN LIVERS

This particular speciality from Piedmont relies heavily on the freshness and good quality of the chicken livers and the quality of the fresh pasta. Tajarin is similar to tagliatelle, but cut more finely.

SERVES 4

150g chicken livers
4 tablespoons unsalted butter
6 tablespoons rich chicken stock
4 tablespoons freshly grated
   Parmesan cheese
2 tablespoons chopped parsley,
   to garnish
Sea salt and freshly ground
   black pepper
PASTA
250g plain white pasta flour, 00,
   plus extra for rolling out
2 eggs
2–3 tablespoons milk

1. Make the pasta dough by kneading together the flour, eggs and milk in a bowl, then continue to make the pasta as described on pages 19–20). Slice into strips about 5mm wide with a sharp knife and set aside.

2. Remove any black or green spots from the chicken livers, as well as any white or yellow traces of fatty tissue. In a large saucepan, melt the butter and quickly fry the livers until well browned. Stir in the stock, remove from the heat and keep warm.

3. Meanwhile, bring a large saucepan of salted water to a rolling boil and add the pasta. Cook for about 5 minutes until al dente (firm to the bite), then drain and transfer to the pan with the chicken livers and seasoning. With two forks, mix together thoroughly.

4. Stir through the Parmesan and transfer to a warmed serving bowl or individual pasta bowls. Serve sprinkled with chopped parsley.

ULTIMATE SPAGHETTI BOLOGNESE

SERVES 4

6 tablespoons olive or vegetable oil

1 onion, peeled and finely chopped

1 carrot, peeled and finely chopped

2 celery sticks, finely chopped

1 garlic clove, peeled and finely
   chopped (optional)

2 tablespoons finely chopped fatty
   prosciutto crudo (or fatty streaky
   bacon)

1 heaped tablespoon dried porcini
   mushrooms, soaked in warm water
   for 15 minutes and then drained
   (optional)

450g lean minced beef

1 large glass of red wine

1 tablespoon tomato purée diluted
   with ½ wine glass of warm water

400g passata (sieved tomatoes) or
   chopped canned tomatoes

Extra stock or water (optional)

400g spaghetti

5 tablespoons freshly grated
   Parmesan cheese, to serve

Sea salt and freshly ground
   black pepper

1. First, heat the oil in a large saucepan and fry the onion, carrot, celery and garlic, if using, together until the onion is soft and transparent. Add the prosciutto crudo, stir and simmer for about 4 minutes until the fat runs and the meat becomes opaque.

2. If using, stir in the drained mushrooms and then add the minced beef. Brown the beef carefully (do not let it go crisp), then pour in the wine and increase the heat to reduce.

3. Stir in the tomato purée and passata or canned tomatoes. Season to taste with salt and pepper, then cover. Simmer very, very slowly for about 2 hours or overnight, if possible (add extra water or stock, if necessary), stirring frequently.

4. When you are ready to eat the dish, reheat the sauce and bring a large saucepan of salted water to a rolling boil. Add the spaghetti and stir once. Cook according to the package directions until al dente (firm to the bite).

5. Drain the pasta and return to the saucepan in which it was cooked. Add the sauce, mix together thoroughly and then transfer to a warmed serving bowl or individual plates.

6. Sprinkle with freshly grated Parmesan cheese and serve at once.

SEDANI WITH PUMPKIN

The name *sedani* refers to celery sticks, which is what these long, narrow and finely ribbed maccheroni look like. Any short, tubular pasta shape, such as ribbed penne, would also be perfect for this dish.

SERVES 4

4 tablespoons extra virgin olive oil

1 large onion, peeled and thinly sliced

120g chopped bacon or pancetta

4 sage leaves

4 tablespoons dry white wine

250g pumpkin, skinned, deseeded and diced

200ml vegetable stock

350g sedani or narrow maccheroni

3 tablespoons finely chopped flat leaf parsley

5 tablespoons freshly grated Parmesan cheese

Fresh bread, to serve

Sea salt and freshly ground black pepper

1. Heat half the oil in a large frying pan and gently fry the onion with the bacon or pancetta and the sage leaves.

2. Add the wine and continue cooking for about 2 minutes, or until the alcohol has evaporated, then add the diced pumpkin. Stir in the vegetable stock and season with salt and pepper. Leave to simmer gently, stirring frequently for about 10 minutes.

3. Meanwhile, bring a large saucepan of salted water to a rolling boil. Add the pasta and stir once. Cover with a lid and return to the boil, then cook, uncovered, until al dente (firm to the bite) according to the package directions.

4. Drain the pasta and add to the pan with the pumpkin sauce. Mix together thoroughly, adding the parsley, the remaining oil and half the cheese over a medium heat for about 5 minutes.

5. Transfer to a warmed serving dish or individual pasta bowls. Sprinkle with the remaining cheese and serve at once with fresh bread.

PASTA TIP

You can also use butternut squash instead of pumpkin. It is a creamier taste and is sometimes more readily available.

TORTELLINI IN BRODO

This classic dish is often part of the Christmas feast in many parts of Italy, especially in the northern regions. When making the pasta, remember that you are not making pastry, so there is no need to take a delicate approach! You could make the soup and filling, and assemble the tortellini the day before to save time (store on a floured tray under a lightly floured cloth in the refrigerator).

SERVES 10

1 large boiling fowl or capon, rinsed
   and ready to cook
3 carrots, topped and tailed
3 onions, peeled and halved
2 celery sticks
2 tomatoes, halved
2 cabbage leaves
1 handful of parsley
4 litres cold water
Freshly grated Parmesan cheese,
   to serve
Sea salt

FILLING

50g unsalted butter
100g diced pork loin
50g diced turkey breast
100g thickly sliced, diced prosciutto
   crudo
100g thickly sliced, diced mortadella
2 eggs, beaten

1. To make the *brodo* (broth), place the bird in a large saucepan with the vegetables, parsley, water and a little salt. Slowly bring to the boil, cover and simmer gently for about 2 hours. Leave to cool in the saucepan. Once cold, lift out the bird and set aside.

2. Strain the liquid through a fine sieve. Leave to stand, then remove any fat that rises to the surface and strain again to make 3.5 litres of soup.

3. Make the filling and pasta, then assemble the tortellini.

4. Bring the *brodo* to a gentle boil and add the tortellini. Simmer until al dente (firm to the bite), about 2–3 minutes, then remove from the heat.

5. Ladle the soup out into individual bowls or transfer to a soup tureen and serve. Note: in Italy, it is normal practice to ask your guests whether they prefer tortellini with more or less brodo and to serve accordingly. Offer freshly grated Parmesan separately at the table.

MAKE THE FILLING

1. Melt the butter in a large saucepan and fry the pork and turkey together, stirring, for 10 minutes. Mince 3 times by hand or process

5 tablespoons freshly grated
Parmesan cheese
A large pinch of grated nutmeg
Sea salt and freshly ground black
pepper

PASTA

350g plain white pasta flour, 00,
plus extra for rolling out
350g fine semolina
7 eggs

once in a food processor together with the prosciutto crudo
and mortadella.

2. Stir in the eggs, seasoning, Parmesan and nutmeg. Mix together
thoroughly. Note: this can be done in a liquidizer or food processor but
be careful not to get too smooth a texture. Set aside until needed.

PASTA AND ASSEMBLY

1. To make the pasta, pile the flour and semolina together on a work
surface and make a well in the centre with your fist.

2. Break the eggs into a large bowl and beat together thoroughly with a
fork. Add to the well and begin to knead roughly with the flour and then
knead together thoroughly until you have a smooth, pliable ball of dough.

3. Leave to rest under a clean cloth or wrap in clingfilm for 20 minutes to
relax the gluten in the flour and make the dough more manageable.

4. On a floured surface, roll out the dough as thinly as possible. Continue
rolling, again and again, until really elastic, smooth and shiny (it should
cool considerably as you work it). When ready, the dough will feel like a
new, wrung-out damp chamois.

5. Proceed to fill the dough with filling, covering the rolled-out pasta
with a slightly damp tea towel to prevent it from drying out as you work.
Cut the pasta into 4cm squares, place about a pinch of filling in the
centre and fold in half. Seal the edges.

6. Hold the triangle between your index and middle finger. Bring the
2 side corners together to form a peaked ring. Hold lightly between your
palms, push your thumb tips into the central hole and push out to form
the tortellini shape.

VEGETARIAN

SPINACH & RICOTTA CANNELLONI

Cannelloni is always popular as a pasta dish. Comforting and easy to make and serve, any number of different fillings can be added, from the most simple to those suitable for sophisticated dinner parties.

SERVES 4

1kg spinach, picked over and rinsed
   in several changes of water
200g fresh ricotta cheese
Pinch of grated nutmeg
8 tablespoons freshly grated
   Parmesan cheese
1 egg
Sea salt and freshly ground
   black pepper

BÉCHAMEL SAUCE

75g unsalted butter
4 level tablespoons plain white flour
600ml cold milk
A pinch of grated nutmeg
A pinch of sea salt

PASTA

400g plain white pasta flour, 00,
   plus extra for rolling out
4 eggs

1. Preheat the oven to 180°C/350°F/Gas Mark 4. Meanwhile, lightly grease a 24cm ovenproof dish with butter.

2. To make the béchamel sauce, melt the butter in a saucepan, then add the flour and mix together until a yellow paste (roux) is formed. Pour in the milk and whisk to prevent lumps forming. Add the salt and nutmeg to taste, then simmer gently for about 15 minutes, stirring constantly.

3. When the sauce is thick enough to coat the back of a spoon, remove from the heat and sprinkle the surface with a little cold water to prevent a skin forming. Set aside until needed.

4. Prepare the fresh pasta (see pages 19–20) and leave to rest while you make the filling.

5. In a large, covered saucepan over low heat, wilt the spinach with the water still clinging to the leaves after rinsing. Drain thoroughly and leave to cool.

6. When the cooked spinach is cool enough to handle, squeeze it dry in your hands, then finely chop. Mix together in a large bowl with the

ricotta. Add the nutmeg, seasoning and half the Parmesan. Blend together with 1 egg and set aside until needed.

7. On a floured surface, roll out the pasta dough as thinly as possible, then cut into rectangles about the size of your palm. Bring a saucepan of salted water to a rolling boil and cook the pasta in batches (about 3).

8. As soon as the pasta rises to the surface of the water, remove with a slotted spoon or fish slice. Lay it carefully in a wide bowl or tray of cold water to prevent the sheets from sticking together. Remove each pasta sheet from the water and drain carefully on kitchen paper.

9. Place about $1\frac{1}{2}$ tablespoons filling on each pasta sheet and roll up with the filling inside to form a cylinder. Continue until the filling and pasta have been used up and arrange the cylinders side by side and seam side down in the ovenproof dish.

10. Cover with béchamel and sprinkle with the remaining Parmesan. Bake for about 20 minutes, or until golden brown and bubbling, then serve the cannelloni at once.

CAVATELLI WITH ROCKET & TOMATO

This recipe works best with the wide-leafed variety of rocket rather than the finer, so-called 'wild' rocket as the leaves tend to maintain their shape better after boiling and their flavour is stronger. Cavatelli are a small, cup-shaped type of pasta typical to southern Italy, but any small shape such as conchiglie will also work well.

SERVES 4

3 handfuls of rocket leaves
7 tablespoons extra virgin olive oil
3 large spring onions, sliced
1 celery stick, rinsed and chopped
1 large garlic clove, peeled
4 large ripe tomatoes, peeled, deseeded and chopped
2 anchovy fillets preserved in oil, drained and chopped (optional)
1 dried red chilli pepper, chopped
350g cavatelli or similar pasta shape
4 tablespoons freshly grated pecorino cheese, to serve

1. First, wash and coarsely chop the rocket.

2. Heat half the oil in a very wide, deep frying pan and fry the spring onions and celery together until softened, stirring frequently. Set aside.

3. Bring a large saucepan of salted water to a rolling boil. Meanwhile, in a separate, smaller frying pan, heat the remaining oil and fry the garlic until golden brown and then discard.

4. Add the tomatoes, anchovies, if using, and chilli to the garlic-scented oil. Fry together gently for about 10 minutes, stirring frequently, then set aside.

5. Cook the pasta and the rocket together in the boiling water according to the pasta package directions until al dente (firm to the bite). Drain and tip into the pan with the spring onion and celery.

6. Mix together to coat the pasta and then transfer to a warmed serving dish. Pour the tomato sauce over the dressed cavatelli. Sprinkle with pecorino and serve at once.

LIGURIAN MACCHERONI WITH VEGETABLES

Of all the regions of Italy, Liguria is the one that best celebrates the use of a variety of fresh herbs and vegetables, as this recipe shows.

SERVES 4

200g peeled and diced potatoes
100g fresh or frozen peas
100g trimmed and diced green beans
2 small carrots, trimmed, peeled
   and diced
400g maccheroni
1 handful of chopped marjoram
   leaves
6 tablespoons extra virgin olive oil
2 tablespoons finely chopped flat leaf
   parsley
3 tablespoons freshly grated
   Parmesan cheese
Sea salt and freshly ground
   black pepper

1. First, rinse all the vegetables, then place in a large saucepan of salted water and bring to the boil. Leave to simmer until half-cooked and then add the maccheroni. Stir once and continue to cook according to the package directions.

2. Two minutes before the pasta is ready, add the chopped marjoram and continue to boil according to the package directions until the pasta is al dente (firm to the bite). Drain and transfer to a warmed serving dish.

3. Add the oil, seasoning and parsley. Mix together thoroughly. Add half the Parmesan and mix again. Sprinkle the remaining cheese on top and serve at once.

BLACK TAGLIATELLE WITH ORANGE PEPPER PESTO

SERVES 6

2 large juicy orange peppers, rinsed
  and dried
1 egg
1 garlic clove, peeled
3 tablespoons chopped parsley
3 tablespoons olive oil
500g black (squid ink) tagliatelle
Freshly grated Parmesan cheese,
  to serve
Sea salt and freshly ground
  black pepper

1. Roast the peppers under a preheated medium grill, in a preheated oven (200°C/400°F/Gas Mark 6) or with a blowtorch or lit gas ring, turning frequently until the skins blacken, about 10 minutes. Wrap in clingfilm or place on a tray and cover with a large bowl to steam, then leave to cool.

2. Meanwhile, bring a large saucepan of salted water to a rolling boil. When the peppers are cool, rub off their external skins and rinse carefully, holding them under a cold, slowly running tap. Afterwards any remaining bits of skin can easily be removed with a sharp knife.

3. Slice the peppers in half and remove the seeds and membrane. Place in a food processor or liquidizer. Add the egg, garlic, parsley, olive oil and seasoning. Whizz together thoroughly to make a smooth orange and green-flecked sauce. Set aside until needed.

4. Tip the pasta into the boiling water. Stir once and return to the boil. Cook according to the package directions until al dente (firm to the bite). Drain and return to the hot saucepan.

5. Add the orange pepper sauce and toss together to thoroughly coat the pasta. Transfer to a plate and serve with freshly grated Parmesan offered separately.

NEAPOLITAN MALTAGLIATI

SERVES 4

300g diced aubergines, skin on
3 tablespoons extra virgin olive oil
1 shallot, peeled and chopped
1 handful of basil leaves, rinsed
   and shredded
300g tomatoes, peeled, deseeded
   and chopped
3 salted anchovies, washed, boned
   and chopped (optional)
350g maltagliati
150g diced mozzarella cheese
5 tablespoons freshly grated
   Parmesan cheese
Sea salt and freshly ground
   black pepper

1. Put the diced aubergines in a colander and sprinkle generously with salt. Place a plate and a heavy weight on top. Put the colander in the sink or over a bowl and leave the aubergines to drain for about 30 minutes. Rinse, pat dry and then set aside.

2. Heat the oil in a large frying pan with the shallot and half the basil. Fry together very gently without allowing the shallot to brown. Add the diced aubergine and cook together, stirring, for 3–4 minutes.

3. Stir in the tomatoes and season with salt and pepper. Simmer for about 20 minutes, stirring frequently and adding a little water, if required.

4. Stir in the remaining basil and the anchovies, if using, then remove from the heat and keep warm.

5. Bring a large saucepan of salted water to a rolling boil and cook the maltagliati according to the package directions until al dente (firm to the bite).

6. Drain and tip the pasta into the pan with the aubergines and tomatoes. Mix together and then add the diced mozzarella and half the Parmesan.

7. Mix together once more and then transfer to a warmed serving dish. Sprinkle with the remaining Parmesan and serve at once.

PASTA WITH PESTO GENOVESE

SERVES 4

250g trenette (the traditional ribbon shape used in Liguria), or bavette or linguine

200g green beans, topped and tailed, then boiled or steamed for about 9 minutes until tender

200g potatoes, peeled, diced and boiled or steamed until tender

Sea salt

PESTO

2–4 large handfuls of basil leaves, rinsed and dried to avoid bruising

A large pinch of rock salt

2–3 garlic cloves, peeled and cut in half (or more, if preferred)

1 generous handful of pine nuts

2–6 tablespoons grated Parmesan or pecorino cheese, or a mixture of half and half

About $\frac{1}{2}$ wine glass of best-quality olive oil

Sea salt and freshly ground black pepper

1. First, bring a large saucepan of salted water to a rolling boil and cook the pasta according to the package directions until al dente (firm to the bite). In the last 3 minutes of cooking time, add the cooked beans and potatoes to heat them through.

2. Drain everything together through a colander, then dress with the prepared pesto (slightly dilute this with a little of the hot pasta cooking water to slake it enough so that it coats the other ingredients easily). Serve at once.

PESTO

1. Place the basil, rock salt and garlic in a mortar and reduce to a smooth green purée.

2. Add the pine nuts and cheese. Blend these in also and then slowly begin to add the oil, a little at a time, until a smooth, creamy texture is reached.

3. Season with salt and pepper, then use as required (see above).

PASTA WITH COURGETTES

Very few ingredients are needed to prepare this lovely, sweet-tasting pasta dish. If the courgettes are juicy and sweet, the end result is always delicious.

SERVES 6

125ml olive oil
200g tender courgettes, sliced
 into discs
500g ruote or eliche
Freshly grated Parmesan cheese,
 to serve
Sea salt and freshly ground
 black pepper

1. Heat the olive oil in a large frying pan and gently fry the courgettes until softened and browned around the edges. Season to taste with salt and pepper. Keep warm.

2. Bring a large saucepan of salted water to a rolling boil and tip in the pasta. Stir once and return to the boil. Cook according to the package directions until al dente (firm to the bite).

3. When the pasta is cooked, drain and transfer to the frying pan with the courgettes and olive oil. Over medium heat, quickly toss together the pasta and courgettes and then transfer to a warmed serving platter. Serve at once with the Parmesan cheese offered separately.

TAGLIOLINI WITH TRUFFLE SHAVINGS

One of the most elegant and special pasta dishes ever created. It is very expensive to buy fresh truffles, especially white, but the flavour is absolutely unforgettable. White truffles are more rare, but they have a more intense flavour, so it is worth the extra effort needed to get hold of them.

SERVES 4

400g fresh tagliolini (very fine ribbons) or spaghetti
6 tablespoons single cream
1 black or white truffle
2 tablespoons freshly grated Parmesan cheese, to serve
Sea salt and freshly ground black pepper

1. Bring a large saucepan of salted water to a rolling boil. Toss in the pasta and give it a good stir, then cover and return to the boil. Remove the lid and boil, uncovered, according to the package directions for about 2 minutes, or until al dente (firm to the bite), then drain.

2. Return the pasta to the saucepan, mix in the single cream and season with a little pepper. Transfer to a warmed serving dish.

3. Shave the truffle over the pasta, then sprinkle with Parmesan and serve at once.

MEZZE PENNE WITH PORCINI MUSHROOMS

Although you could of course use any kind of short pasta shape for this dish, the original recipe does call for half (mezze) penne – in other words, half the length but the same width as regular penne.

SERVES 4

4 tablespoons extra virgin olive oil
300g fresh porcini (cep) mushrooms, cleaned and sliced (see Pasta tip)
2 garlic cloves, lightly crushed
A large pinch of dried oregano
400g mezze penne
Freshly grated Parmesan cheese, to serve
Sea salt and freshly ground black pepper

1. Heat the olive oil in a large frying pan, then add the mushrooms and garlic. Fry over a moderate heat, stirring frequently, for about 5 minutes.

2. Remove the garlic, add seasoning and sprinkle over the oregano. Continue to cook gently over a low heat, covered, for about 10 minutes.

3. Meanwhile, bring a large saucepan of salted water to a rolling boil. Add the pasta and stir once. Return to the boil and cook the pasta according to the package directions until al dente (firm to the bite). Drain and return to the cooking saucepan.

4. Pour over the mushrooms, mix together thoroughly and transfer to a warmed serving dish or individual pasta bowls. Serve at once, with freshly grated Parmesan offered separately.

PASTA TIP
In the absence of porcini, use any other strong-flavoured wild or cultivated mushrooms instead.

L'ARRABBIATA

You can vary the heat in this classic sauce by adding or reducing the amount of chilli. Just remember that the smaller the chilli, the hotter it will be!

SERVES 6

4 tablespoons extra virgin olive oil

4 garlic cloves, peeled and finely chopped

1–4 dried red chillies, chopped, crushed or used whole according to preference

500g chopped canned tomatoes, drained, if necessary

400g penne

1 teaspoon chopped parsley, to garnish

Sea salt

1. In a large frying pan, heat the olive oil and fry the garlic and chilli together until slightly blackened. Discard and stir the tomatoes into the pan. Season with salt and simmer for about 20 minutes until glossy and thickened.

2. Meanwhile, bring a large saucepan of salted water to a rolling boil and add the penne. Stir once, cover and return to the boil. Cook according to the package directions until al dente (firm to the bite). Drain and return to the saucepan.

3. Pour over the sauce and toss to combine. Transfer to a warmed serving dish and sprinkle with parsley just before serving.

PASTA TIP

Grated cheese is not normally served with this recipe, however, if you or your guests insist, it has to be aged, peppery pecorino.

COLD PASTA SALAD WITH PEPPERS

The combination of fresh basil with the roasted peppers is particularly delicious, especially with the hint of hot sharpness given by the mustard in the dressing.

SERVES 4

4 large ripe tomatoes
1 red pepper
1 yellow pepper
Juice of 1 lemon
7 tablespoons extra virgin olive oil
1 teaspoon Italian mustard (Savora),
    or use French mustard
350g ribbed penne
1 large handful of basil leaves, rinsed
    and finely shredded
Sea salt and freshly ground
    black pepper

1. Preheat the grill to medium or the oven to 180°C/350°F/Gas Mark 4.

2. Blanch the tomatoes in a large saucepan of boiling water for 2–4 minutes, then skin and deseed them. Roughly chop into chunks.

3. Place the peppers on a baking sheet and roast under the grill or in the oven until browned and wrinkled. Transfer to a bowl, cover with a sheet of clingfilm to steam until cooled, then remove from the bowl and peel away the skins. Deseed and cut into rough chunks.

4. In a small bowl, mix together the lemon juice with the salt, oil and mustard to form a thick and creamy dressing.

5. Bring a saucepan of salted water to a rolling boil and then cook the pasta until al dente (firm to the bite) according to the package directions. Drain and rinse thoroughly under cold running water.

6. Transfer the pasta to a large salad bowl. Add the tomatoes, peppers and dressing, then mix together thoroughly. Sprinkle with basil and adjust the seasoning.

7. Chill for at least 1 hour before serving to allow the flavours to develop.

LINGUINE WITH ASPARAGUS & TOMATO

You can use long pasta such as linguine, bucatini or spaghetti for this recipe, or short pasta like penne, if you prefer. Frozen asparagus can be used instead of fresh for this sauce.

SERVES 4

1kg fresh green asparagus
4 tablespoons olive oil
2 garlic cloves, peeled
500g canned tomatoes, deseeded and chopped
400g linguine
Freshly grated Parmesan cheese, to serve
Sea salt and freshly ground black pepper

1. First, rinse and trim the asparagus, then cut into short sections.

2. Heat the olive oil in a frying pan and gently fry the garlic until golden brown and then discard.

3. Add the asparagus to the garlic-scented oil. Cook gently until softened, turning occasionally. Add the tomatoes, stirring to combine. Season to taste with salt and pepper and cook for 10–15 minutes.

4. Meanwhile, bring a large saucepan of salted water to a rolling boil and add the linguine to the water. Stir once and then boil the pasta according to the package directions until al dente (firm to the bite).

5. Drain the pasta and return to the cooking saucepan. Pour over the asparagus sauce and mix together thoroughly.

6. Transfer to a warm serving dish and serve at once, with the Parmesan offered separately.

LASAGNA WITH PESTO & POTATOES

SERVES 4

1 packet fresh lasagna (or
   see pages 34–5)
3 medium potatoes, peeled
3 tablespoons unsalted butter,
   plus extra for greasing
3½ tablespoons plain white flour
600ml milk
4 tablespoons Pesto (see page 67,
   or use readymade)
5 tablespoons freshly grated
   Parmesan cheese
Sea salt and freshly ground
   black pepper

1. Preheat the oven to 190°C/375°F/Gas Mark 5. Meanwhile, blanch the sheets of lasagna according to the package directions to soften them. Lay out on a work surface until ready to use (do not overlap or they will stick together).

2. Boil the potatoes in salted water until soft, about 15 minutes, then thinly slice and set aside.

3. Melt the butter in a saucepan until it foams, then add the flour and stir vigorously until a smooth paste (roux) is formed.

4. Add the milk and mix thoroughly. Simmer gently, stirring frequently, until the sauce thickens and you can no longer taste the flour. Stir in half the pesto and season. Add about half the Parmesan and stir again.

5. Lightly butter a 20cm square ovenproof dish and spread a layer of sauce across the base. Cover with a layer of potatoes and then add another layer of sauce. Dot with the reserved pesto.

6. Cover with sheets of lasagna, then another layer of sauce and more pesto. Sprinkle with Parmesan and repeat, finishing with a final layer of sauce.

7. Sprinkle with the remaining Parmesan and place in the centre of the oven to bake for about 20 minutes, or until bubbling hot and golden. Leave to stand for about 5 minutes to firm up before serving.

CONCHIGLIE WITH SPINACH & CREAM

Although you can use any type of pasta you like for this sauce, the cup shape of this particular pasta holds the creamy sauce perfectly. This is a great sauce, with a wonderful colour.

SERVES 4

1kg spinach leaves
400g conchiglie
8 tablespoons single cream
6 tablespoons freshly grated
   Parmesan cheese
1/4 teaspoon grated nutmeg
1 tablespoon butter
Sea salt and freshly ground
   black pepper

1. Rinse the spinach thoroughly, then cram into a large saucepan with the water just clinging to the leaves. Put the lid on top and place over moderate heat for about 5 minutes, or until the leaves have collapsed.

2. Drain well, squeezing out any excess liquid, then set aside.

3. Bring a large saucepan of salted water to a rolling boil. Toss in the pasta, stir well, cover and return to the boil. Remove the lid and boil until al dente (firm to the bite) according to the package directions.

4. Meanwhile, put the cooked spinach in a food processor with the cream and Parmesan. Whizz to make a smooth, green cream, then transfer to a bowl. Stir in the nutmeg and season to taste.

5. Drain the pasta and return to the saucepan. Add the butter and toss together thoroughly. Pour over the sauce and toss once more, then transfer to a warmed serving bowl and serve at once.

PASTA WITH BROCCOLI, PINE NUTS & CHILLI

A deliciously spicy pasta dish with plenty of crunch – add more chilli if you like it a little bit hotter.

SERVES 4

250g tiny broccoli florets
400g pasta of your choice, such
   as pennette or maccheroncini
4 tablepoons chilli oil
1 dried red chilli pepper, whole or
   crushed, according to preference
1 garlic clove, peeled and lightly
   crushed
1 handful of pine nuts
Sea salt

1. Bring a small saucepan of lightly salted water to the boil. Add the broccoli and leave to simmer for about 4 minutes or until just tender. Drain and set aside.

2. Bring a large saucepan of salted water to a rolling boil. Toss in the pasta and stir well. Cover and return to the boil. Remove the lid and boil until al dente (firm to the bite) according to the package directions.

3. Meanwhile, heat the chilli oil in a large frying pan with the chilli pepper and garlic until the oil is just smoking.

4. Remove the chilli and garlic from the oil, then add the pine nuts and broccoli. Heat through, stirring frequently. Season with salt only if necessary and keep warm.

5. Drain the pasta and add to the ingredients in the pan. Toss together thoroughly, then transfer to a warm platter and serve at once.

PAPPARDELLE WITH MUSHROOM SAUCE

SERVES 4

4 large tablespoons olive oil

3 garlic cloves, peeled and finely
chopped (or crushed or puréed)

12 large tomatoes, peeled, deseeded
and coarsely chopped (or 10 canned
plum tomatoes, drained, deseeded
and squeezed dry)

1 handful of dried porcini mushrooms
(soaked in hand-hot water for
20 minutes and then drained),
or 300g fresh porcini (or similar
full-flavoured mushrooms),
cleaned and sliced

400g pappardelle

2 tablespoons chopped flat leaf
parsley

A knob of unsalted butter

Freshly grated Parmesan cheese,
to serve (optional)

Sea salt and freshly ground
black pepper

1. In a large saucepan, heat the oil with the garlic for about 5 minutes, stirring frequently. Add the tomatoes and stir thoroughly.

2. Add the mushrooms and seasoning. Stir gently and cook slowly for about 40 minutes, or until the sauce becomes creamy and the mushrooms are very soft.

3. Meanwhile, bring a large saucepan of salted water to a rolling boil. Add the pasta and stir once. Return to the boil and then simmer until al dente (firm to the bite) according to the package directions. Drain and return to the cooking saucepan.

4. Sprinkle the sauce with freshly chopped parsley and stir through with a knob of butter. Pour over the pasta and mix well.

5. Transfer to a warmed serving platter or individual plates. Serve at once with freshly grated Parmesan offered separately, if liked.

ORECCHIETTE WITH BROCCOLI & TOMATO

This recipe calls for salted, hard-grating ricotta cheese. If this proves hard to find, use a strong hard-grating pecorino instead.

SERVES 4

750g sprouting broccoli
2 salted anchovies (optional)
350g orecchiette
4 tablespoons extra virgin olive oil
1 garlic clove, lightly crushed
200g tomatoes, peeled, deseeded and chopped
3 tablespoons freshly grated salted ricotta cheese
Sea salt and freshly ground black pepper

1. Divide the broccoli into small florets, removing the hard stalks. Rinse and set aside until needed.

2. If using, rinse and remove the bones from the anchovies, then finely chop.

3. Bring a large saucepan of salted water to a rolling boil and then add the orecchiette and cook until al dente (firm to the bite) according to the package directions.

4. Meanwhile, 5 minutes before the pasta is ready, add the broccoli florets and continue cooking.

5. Fry the oil and garlic together over a medium heat until the garlic is golden brown. Discard the garlic and add the anchovies to the pan. Stir and melt the anchovies, then add the tomatoes. Season and leave to simmer for 5 minutes.

6. Drain the pasta and return to the cooking saucepan. Pour over the sauce and mix together well with half the ricotta.

7. Transfer to a warmed serving dish. Sprinkle with the remaining cheese and serve at once.

PASTA WITH BLACK & GREEN GARLICKY OLIVE SAUCE

Feel free to choose your own pasta shape, but ruote work very well with this sauce and look pretty, too. Because the sauce is cold, the dish is not piping hot, which makes it ideal for summer eating.

SERVES 4

400g dried pasta of your choice
15 black olives, pitted
15 green olives, pitted
2 garlic cloves
4 tablespoons olive oil
1 tablespoon soft white breadcrumbs
1 teaspoon lemon juice
2 tablespoons chopped fresh parsley,
    to garnish
Sea salt and freshly ground
    black pepper

1. Bring a large saucepan of salted water to a rolling boil. Add the pasta and stir well. Cover and return to the boil. Cook according to the package directions until al dente (firm to the bite).

2. Meanwhile, put the olives and garlic in the bowl of a food processor. Whizz, gradually pouring in the oil, to make a fairly smooth paste. Alternatively, pound in a pestle and mortar.

3. Add the breadcrumbs and season with salt and pepper to taste. Finish off by adding the lemon juice and whizzing for just a few more seconds.

4. Drain the pasta and return to the saucepan. Pour over the olive sauce and toss together to coat well (add a little more oil if the sauce is too dry).

5. Transfer to a warmed serving platter. Sprinkle with parsley and serve.

PASTA ALLA NORMA

SERVES 4

2 large, long aubergines, sliced
   lengthways
1 onion, peeled and quartered
1 carrot, scraped
1 celery stick, rinsed
1 garlic clove, peeled
500g ripe, juicy, sweet fresh tomatoes
   (or equivalent premium canned
   tomatoes)
600ml vegetable oil for deep-frying
400g maccheroni, penne or sedani
4 tablespoons extra virgin olive oil
About 12 small basil sprigs or large
   leaves of basil
6 tablespoons freshly grated salted
   ricotta or pecorino cheese, to serve
Sea salt and freshly ground
   black pepper
(See photograph of dish on page 58,
   top left)

1. Layer the aubergine slices in a wide colander, sprinkling each one with sea salt. Cover tightly with a plate, put a weight on top, then place the colander over a basin and drain out the bitter juices for about 1 hour.

2. Meanwhile, put the onion, carrot, celery, garlic and tomatoes in a heavy-based saucepan. Cover with a lid and place over low heat to slowly cook in their juices for about 40 minutes, or until softened.

3. Push the softened vegetables through a food mill or process until puréed, then return the sauce to the heat to boil again until reduced to a thick texture. Remove from the heat, season to taste and set aside.

4. Rinse and pat dry the aubergine slices on kitchen paper. Cut into neat dice. Heat the vegetable oil until sizzling hot and fry the aubergine until soft and shiny, about 10 minutes. Drain on kitchen paper and keep warm.

5. Bring a large saucepan of salted water to the boil. Add the pasta, stir once and boil until al dente (firm to the bite) according to the package directions. Meanwhile, reheat the tomato sauce and stir in the olive oil, then remove from the heat.

6. Drain the pasta and return it to the hot saucepan. To assemble the dish, add a little tomato sauce to the pasta (just enough to coat lightly). Arrange the pasta in a mound on a warmed platter and pour the remaining sauce over the top so that it trickles down.

7. Sprinkle hot, fried aubergine cubes down the sides of the pasta and arrange basil sprigs so they are half-buried in the tomato sauce. Sprinkle cheese over the top and serve at once.

PENNE WITH PEA SAUCE

This is a very different pasta sauce, resulting in a refreshing summertime recipe. You could use the same quantity of fresh or frozen cooked peas, if you prefer.

SERVES 4

1 x 400g can peas, drained
300ml vegetable stock
5 mint leaves
4 celery leaves
A few drops of Tabasco sauce
6 tablespoons extra virgin olive oil
1 small red onion, peeled and finely
   sliced
350g penne
1 small bunch of fresh watercress,
   rinsed and trimmed
50g peppered pecorino cheese,
   finely shaved
Sea salt and freshly ground
   black pepper

1. Put the peas in the bowl of a food processor, together with the vegetable stock, mint, celery leaves, Tabasco and 5 tablespoons of the oil, and season with salt and pepper. Process until smooth and creamy, then transfer to a small bowl.

2. Leave the onion to soak in cold water until required. Meanwhile, bring a large saucepan of salted water to a rolling boil. Add the pasta and cook until al dente (firm to the bite). Drain and return to the cooking saucepan.

3. Pour over the pea sauce, drained red onion slices and sprinkle with watercress and pecorino. Mix together well.

4. Transfer to a warmed serving dish. Drizzle with the remaining olive oil, sprinkle with pepper and serve at once.

PASTA & FAGIOLI

There are so many recipes for this very dense pasta soup – each and every region of Italy seems to have their own version. Basically, the recipe is always more or less the same, with a few variations such as the addition of tomato purée, other vegetables (courgettes, leeks, pumpkin, tomatoes, green beans and peas), herbs, pancetta, chilli or sometimes a different kind of bean such as borlotti, cannellini or lamon. For vegetarians, simply leave out the pancetta or prosciutto.

SERVES 4

300g canned or dried cannellini or
    borlotti beans
75g fatty pancetta or prosciutto
    (optional)
3 tablespoons olive oil
1 onion, chopped
1 large carrot, chopped
1 large celery stick, chopped
1 litre good meat or vegetable stock
150g small soup pasta, such as Ave
    Marie, cannolicchi, stelline or risoni
Sea salt and freshly ground
    black pepper
TO SERVE
Extra virgin olive oil
Freshly grated Parmesan cheese

1. If using canned beans, drain and set aside. Soak dried or fresh beans overnight in cold water, then drain and rinse. Boil quickly in salted water for 5 minutes to remove the natural toxins. Drain and rinse again. Cover with fresh water and simmer gently until tender, about 40 minutes.

2. Having prepared the beans, fry the pancetta or prosciutto in a large frying pan, if using, with the olive oil, onion, carrot and celery until the vegetables are softened.

3. Add the beans and stir well to combine. Stir in the stock and simmer slowly until the beans are almost falling apart. Add the pasta and cook until al dente (firm to the bite) according to the package directions.

4. Season to taste and serve warm, drizzled with a little extra virgin oil and with a light sprinkling of freshly grated Parmesan.

COLD PASTA WITH VEGETABLES

This is a wonderful pasta dish for hot summer days. Lots of lovely flavours and different textures and colours make it look as delicious as it tastes. Taglierini are long, fine ribbons of egg pasta.

SERVES 4

1 carrot, peeled and sliced into thin
   sticks
Green skin of 1 large courgette, sliced
   into thin batons
1 red onion, baked whole in the oven
   (20 minutes at 180°C/350°F/Gas
   Mark 4), then cooled, peeled and
   thinly sliced
1 large tomato, rinsed, deseeded and
   sliced into strips
5 tablespoons extra virgin olive oil
350g taglierini, tagliatelle or tagliolini
2–3 tablespoons shaved Parmesan
   cheese
Sea salt and freshly ground
   black pepper

1. Cook the carrot sticks in boiling salted water for 10 minutes. Refresh in iced water. Repeat with the courgette skin, but cook for 5 minutes in this case. Drain once cold.

2. Put all the vegetables in a deep bowl with the oil and gently toss.

3. Bring a large saucepan of salted water to a rolling boil. Cook the pasta until al dente (firm to the bite), then drain and tip over the vegetables in the bowl.

4. Mix together thoroughly, then add the cheese (reserve a few shavings to garnish) and mix again to combine well.

5. Season with lots of freshly ground pepper and sprinkle with the remaining cheese shavings just before serving the pasta.

PASTA WITH GREEN OLIVE PÂTÉ & WALNUTS

This is a really quick and simple supper dish. You could use black olive pâté if green is unavailable, though to my mind the green version works best.

SERVES 4

400g conchiglie or fusilli
1 x 200g jar green olive pâté
100g shelled walnuts, chopped
2–3 tablespoons extra virgin olive oil
100g freshly grated Parmesan cheese
3 tablespoons chopped flat leaf
   parsley, to garnish
Sea salt

1. Bring a large saucepan of salted water to a rolling boil. Add the pasta and stir once. Cover and return to the boil, then remove the lid and continue cooking according to the package directions until al dente (firm to the bite).

2. Turn off the heat, drain the pasta and return to the same cooking saucepan. Add the olive pâté and mix together thoroughly.

3. Stir in the walnuts, oil and half the cheese. Mix again and then transfer to a warmed serving bowl or individual warmed plates. Sprinkle with the remaining Parmesan and parsley. Serve at once.

BLACK TAGLIOLINI WITH OLIVE OIL & GARLIC

This classic combination of coating pasta with just a hot oil and garlic dressing takes on a new twist when you use black squid ink pasta instead of plain white pasta. If you like spicy food, add one whole dried chilli (or more) to the oil with the garlic and discard once the garlic has browned.

SERVES 4

400g black tagliolini or tagliatelle (squid ink pasta), or use yellow tagliatelle or green spinach tagliatelle

6 tablespoons extra virgin olive oil

4 garlic cloves, peeled and lightly crushed

5 teaspoons chopped parsley, to garnish

Sea salt and freshly ground black pepper

1. Bring a large saucepan of salted water to a rolling boil. Toss in the pasta, stir and boil for about 2 minutes until al dente (firm to the bite), then drain thoroughly.

2. Meanwhile, heat the olive oil with the garlic in a large frying pan until the garlic is golden brown and then discard.

3. Pour the hot flavoured oil over the pasta and toss together to thoroughly coat. Season to taste, then sprinkle with chopped parsley and serve at once.

SPAGHETTI SALAD WITH MINT & OLIVES

There are lots of different variations on the pasta salad theme, but this is one of the tastiest and perhaps most unusual of combinations.

SERVES 4

1 small bunch of mint, rinsed and chopped
2 garlic cloves, peeled
8 tablespoons extra virgin olive oil
8 tablespoons freshly squeezed orange juice
12 black olives, pitted and coarsely chopped
2 canned anchovies in olive oil, drained and chopped (optional)
8 small mushrooms preserved in olive oil
350g spaghetti
Sea salt and freshly ground black pepper

1. Roughly crush together the mint and garlic (use a pestle and mortar, or the flat of a heavy knife on a chopping board). Heat 6 tablespoons of the oil in a frying pan and fry the garlic until pungent and softened.

2. Remove from the heat and add the orange juice, olives, anchovies, if using, and mushrooms. Mix together and season well.

3. Bring a large saucepan of salted water to a rolling boil. Add the pasta and cook until al dente (firm to the bite) according to the package directions. Drain and rinse in very cold water.

4. Transfer the pasta to a bowl and mix through 1 tablespoon of the olive oil to prevent the strands from sticking together.

5. Pour over the sauce and mix together thoroughly until the sauce is well distributed through the pasta.

6. Chill in the refrigerator for at least 1 hour (or overnight if you have time) until ready to serve. To serve, add the last spoonful of oil and toss again just before serving.

BAVETTE WITH ALMOND PESTO

This delicious and very different pesto is not only marvellous on pasta but also especially tasty used as a stuffing inside chicken breasts. Brush with oil and roast or grill.

SERVES 6

6 garlic cloves
1 large handful of basil leaves
150g blanched almonds, roughly chopped
4 ripe tomatoes, peeled and chopped
6 tablespoons olive oil
400g bavette or spaghetti
Sea salt and freshly ground black pepper

1. In a mortar, pound the garlic, 1 teaspoon salt and the basil leaves. Add the almonds, little by little, and then the tomatoes.

2. When all the ingredients are reduced to a pulp, stir in the oil and season with black pepper. Set aside until needed.

3. Meanwhile, bring a large saucepan of salted water to a rolling boil and cook the pasta until al dente (firm to the bite) according to the package directions. Drain and toss in a serving bowl with the pesto until evenly coated, then serve at once.

PASTA TIP
The pesto can be made in a food processor, in which case the oil should be added at the very beginning to make the process smoother and easier; also to avoid puréeing the almonds. Decanted into a clean jar, it will keep for about 1 month in the refrigerator, but make sure the surface is kept coated with olive oil.

PASTA SALAD WITH ARTICHOKES

If you love the taste of artichokes, then this pasta salad will be a winner for you. It's especially good if the mayonnaise is freshly homemade.

SERVES 6

6 fresh artichokes, trimmed and prepared down to the hearts

500g short pasta, such as penne or conchiglie

1 generous tablespoon extra virgin olive oil

4 tablespoons mayonnaise

3 hard-boiled eggs, peeled and sliced, to garnish

Sea salt and freshly ground black pepper

1. Boil the artichoke hearts in salted water for about 10 minutes until tender. Drain and cut into small pieces about the same size or slightly smaller than the pasta.

2. Bring a large saucepan of salted water to a rolling boil. Cook the pasta until al dente (firm to the bite) according to the package directions and then drain.

3. Refresh the pasta under cold running water, drain and transfer to a bowl. Mix lightly with the olive oil to prevent sticking.

4. Stir in the cooked artichoke pieces and the mayonnaise. Mix together well, season and serve at once, garnished with slices of hard-boiled egg.

SPAGHETTINI WITH SULTANAS & PINE NUTS

This slightly sweet Venetian pasta dish is steeped in tradition. Although a little unusual, it tastes delicious and deserves to be tried!

SERVES 4

100g sultanas
400g spaghettini or spaghetti
100g pine nuts
4–6 tablespoons olive oil
A pinch of ground cinnamon
Sea salt

TO SERVE

Freshly grated Parmesan cheese,
   to serve
Crusty french bread

1. Preheat the oven to 200°C/400°F/Gas Mark 6. Meanwhile, put the sultanas in a heatproof bowl. Cover with warm water and soak for 10 minutes until plump. Drain and pat dry with kitchen paper.

2. Bring a large saucepan of salted water to a rolling boil. Toss in the spaghettini, forcing it down into the water. Stir well and cover. Return to the boil, remove the lid and boil according to the package directions until al dente (firm to the bite).

3. Meanwhile, mix the sultanas with the pine nuts.

4. Drain the pasta and return to the cooking saucepan. Pour over the oil and toss together to coat. Add the pine nuts, sultanas and cinnamon. Toss together and transfer to an ovenproof dish.

5. Bake for 5 minutes, or until the top is just crisp. Serve at once with grated Parmesan, offered separately.

PENNE WITH VODKA SAUCE

This is a very popular, modern classic pasta dish in Italy, often served late in the evening as a sort of mid-party refreshment.

SERVES 4

400g penne
2 tablespoons unsalted butter
1 fresh red chilli pepper, deseeded
   and finely chopped
2 tablespoons concentrated tomato
   purée
9 tablespoons single or double cream
4 tablespoons vodka
2 tablespoons freshly grated
   Parmesan cheese, to serve
Sea salt and freshly ground
   black pepper

1. Bring a large saucepan of salted water to a rolling boil. Add the penne and cook according to the package directions until al dente (firm to the bite).

2. Meanwhile, melt the butter in a wide frying pan and fry the chilli for about 5 minutes. Add the tomato purée and mix together well.

3. After 3 or 4 minutes stir in the cream. Bring to the boil and then remove from the heat. Stir in the vodka and set aside until needed, but keep warm.

4. Drain the cooked pasta and tip into the cooking saucepan with the sauce. Mix together over high heat for 3 minutes or so (taste to check). Adjust the seasoning, transfer to a warmed dish, sprinkle with the Parmesan and serve at once.

GREEN TAGLIATELLE WITH ROASTED PEPPERS

SERVES 4

2 large, sweet juicy red peppers
3 garlic cloves, peeled and puréed
$\frac{1}{2}$ teaspoon anchovy paste (optional)
About 8 tablespoons extra virgin
   olive oil
4 tablespoons chopped flat leaf
   parsley
400g green spinach tagliatelle
Sea salt and freshly ground
   black pepper

1. Preheat the grill and when hot, place the peppers on the grill tray. Turn frequently under the heat until the skins blacken and become wrinkly.

2. Remove from the heat, turn off the grill and wrap the peppers in individual plastic sandwich bags. Leave until completely cold, then take out of the bags and remove the skins.

3. Slice the peppers in half and remove the seeds and membranes. Cut into strips and arrange flat on a plate set over simmering water to warm the peppers without cooking them.

4. Bring a large saucepan of salted water to a rolling boil. Meanwhile, whisk the garlic purée with salt, anchovy paste, if using, oil, parsley and pepper. Set aside.

5. Add the tagliatelle to the boiling water, stir once and return to the boil. Cook according to the package directions until al dente (firm to the bite).

6. Transfer the peppers to a large, warmed serving bowl and coat with half the dressing. Drain the pasta and return to the cooking saucepan. Pour over the remaining dressing, toss together to combine and then pour the pasta on top of the dressed peppers. Mix together thoroughly and serve.

FISH & SHELLFISH

BAKED PASTA WITH MACKEREL & TOMATO

SERVES 4–6

500g maccheroni

5 tablespoons extra virgin olive oil, plus extra for greasing

300g mackerel fillets, skinned

2 garlic cloves, peeled and finely chopped

400g canned tomatoes, chopped

1 tablespoon capers, rinsed and chopped

2 tablespoons black olives, pitted

1 teaspoon dried oregano

50g mozzarella cheese, finely chopped

2 tablespoons fresh breadcrumbs

Dried oregano, to garnish

Sea salt and freshly ground black pepper

PASTA TIP
The recipe calls for the much-underrated mackerel, although other oily fish would also work well.

1. Preheat the oven to 190°C/375°F/Gas Mark 5. Meanwhile, bring a large saucepan of salted water to a rolling boil. Cook the pasta until al dente (firm to the bite) according to the package directions. Drain and briefly rinse under cold running water.

2. Transfer the drained pasta to a large mixing bowl and add 2 tablespoons of the olive oil. Mix together thoroughly and set aside.

3. Cut the fish into neat squares and rinse under cold running water, then pat dry with kitchen paper.

4. In a separate saucepan, fry the garlic and the remaining oil together (reserve a little for drizzling) for about 4 minutes until the garlic is golden, then add the fish. Stir briefly to coat the fish in the oil and garlic.

5. Stir in the canned tomatoes and leave to simmer for 10 minutes, stirring frequently. Sprinkle in the capers, olives and oregano. Adjust the seasoning and simmer for a further 10 minutes.

6. Mix the sauce and pasta together, then transfer to a greased ovenproof dish. Scatter with mozzarella, sprinkle with breadcrumbs and add a final drizzle of olive oil.

7. Bake in the oven for 10–15 minutes, or until crisp and golden on top. Leave to stand for 5 minutes to firm up before serving.

BUCATINI WITH TUNA

This is a very quick, storecupboard favourite. Make sure the canned tuna is of good quality for the very best results.

SERVES 4

400g bucatini
200g canned tuna in olive oil, drained
1 tablespoon anchovy paste
3 tablespoons fish stock or water
3 tablespoons extra virgin olive oil
2 tablespoons chopped parsley
Sea salt and freshly ground
   black pepper

1. Bring a large saucepan of salted water to a rolling boil. Add the bucatini, stir and continue to cook according to the package directions until al dente (firm to the bite).

2. Meanwhile, whizz the drained tuna in a food processor with the anchovy paste, fish stock or water, half the olive oil and seasoning.

3. Drain the pasta and return to the cooking saucepan. Add the remaining oil and half the chopped parsley. Mix together, add the tuna sauce and mix again.

4. Adjust the seasoning and transfer to a warmed serving dish or individual pasta bowls. Sprinkle with the remaining parsley and serve.

SPAGHETTI WITH SQUID INK

SERVES 4–6

6 medium-sized whole cleaned squid
(your fishmonger can do this
for you)
4 tablespoons olive oil
2 or 3 garlic cloves, peeled and
lightly crushed
3 tablespoons chopped parsley
100ml dry white wine
3 tablespoons concentrated
tomato purée
400g spaghetti
2–3 tablespoons squid ink
Sea salt and freshly ground
black pepper

1. First, wash the squid carefully in cold water and cut into small cubes. Finely chop the tentacles. Rinse and dry the fish very thoroughly.

2. Heat the olive oil in a large saucepan with the garlic. Fry the garlic until brown and then discard.

3. Add the squid, parsley and plenty of black pepper. Stir together and simmer, covered, for about 45 minutes.

4. Pour over the white wine and add the tomato purée. Stir to thoroughly combine and simmer, uncovered, for about 20 minutes, then lower the heat further and cover. Continue cooking for a further 30 minutes, occasionally adding a little hot water to dilute the sauce.

5. About half an hour before you want to eat, bring a large pot of salted water to the boil. Toss in the pasta, stir and continue to cook until al dente (firm to the bite) according to the package directions. Drain very thoroughly and return to the pot.

6. At the same time as the pasta is added to the boiling water, put the ink sacs into the sauce and stir it all together.

7. Pour the sauce over the cooked pasta and mix together thoroughly. Cover and leave to stand for about 5 minutes, then turn out onto a warmed platter and serve at once.

PUTTANESCA

This famous and much-loved sauce is named for the Ladies of the Night, who frequent some of the more disreputable areas of Rome. Depending on how much flavour you like, garlic can be treated in all sorts of ways. For the mildest taste, crush lightly and remove from the oil when golden brown. If you prefer a stronger taste, peel and mince the garlic to a purée, then add to the oil.

SERVES 4

8 tablespoons extra virgin olive oil
1 garlic clove, finely chopped, or cut in half or whole (crushed or uncrushed) according to preference
3–5 anchovy fillets (salted or canned in oil, rinsed and dried)
1–4 small dried red chilli peppers, finely chopped
1 tablespoon rinsed and dried salted capers, roughly chopped
200g chopped canned tomatoes
A very large pinch of dried oregano
120ml dry white wine
1 handful of stoned black olives
400g penne or spaghetti
1 generous handful of flat leaf parsley, roughly chopped
Freshly grated Parmesan cheese, to garnish
Sea salt and freshly ground black pepper

1. In a large frying pan, heat half the oil and fry the garlic with the anchovy fillets and dried chilli pepper until the anchovy dissolves.

2. Add the capers and the tomatoes and stir together thoroughly. Simmer for a few minutes and then add the oregano, seasoning, wine and olives.

3. Stir and leave to simmer gently for at least 15 minutes, though longer will do no harm.

4. Meanwhile, bring a saucepan of salted water to a rolling boil and cook the pasta (traditionally penne or spaghetti) according to the package directions until al dente (firm to the bite).

5. Spoon the sauce over the cooked pasta and toss together with the remaining olive oil and the chopped parsley, reserving a little parsley to garnish.

6. Arrange on a serving platter, garnish with freshly grated Parmesan and the reserved parsley and serve at once.

FARFALLE WITH PEPPERS & PRAWNS

This is a lovely summer pasta dish, as it is only just warm and is equally delicious cold. It looks pretty, is quite low in fat and tastes wonderful.

SERVES 4

2 yellow peppers and 1 red pepper

300g farfalle

300g cooked prawns

1 small handful of mixed parsley, basil and thyme, finely chopped

5 tablespoons best-quality extra virgin olive oil

Sea salt and freshly ground black pepper

PASTA TIP

Farfalle are those butterfly bow shapes of pasta, which are available in many different sizes. When cooking them, make sure they are tender all the way through to the very middle of the bow, where the pasta is doubled over to create the shape.

1. Preheat the oven to 190°C/375°F/Gas Mark 5.

2. Put the peppers on a baking sheet, then roast in the oven until well browned. Remove and transfer into a large bowl. Cover the bowl tightly with clingfilm and leave to steam and cool.

3. Meanwhile, bring a large saucepan of salted water to a rolling boil. Add the farfalle to the boiling water, stir once and return to the boil. Cook until al dente (firm to the bite) according to the package directions.

4. Once the peppers have cooled, remove them from the bowl, skin and deseed them, then cut into small strips.

5. Put the strips of pepper into a large bowl with the prawns, chopped herbs and olive oil. Season with salt and pepper and mix together.

6. Drain the pasta, tip it into the bowl with the peppers and prawns, and mix together. Adjust the seasoning and serve at once.

BAVETTE WITH MONKFISH

Monkfish is a wonderfully easy fish to cook, as it keeps its shape really well and stays nice and firm, giving the finished dish plenty of texture.

SERVES 4

300g monkfish tail
100g sardines, scaled and gutted
5 tablespoons olive oil
1 garlic clove, peeled and finely
    chopped
2 tablespoons finely chopped celery
4 tablespoons cooking brandy
3 tablespoons fish stock
3 ripe tomatoes, peeled and coarsely
    chopped
500g bavette
Sea salt and freshly ground
    black pepper

1. Trim and cube the monkfish tail, discarding the cartilage.

2. Rinse and remove the spine from the sardine fillets. Chop until reduced to a coarse mince.

3. Heat the oil and fry the garlic and celery together in the pan until softened, then add the fish. Fry together until well browned, add the brandy and burn off the alcohol. Stir in the fish stock and the tomatoes, then season with salt and pepper.

4. Cook the fish for about 10 minutes longer, stirring occasionally, then remove from the heat until required. Keep warm.

5. Bring a large saucepan of salted water to a rolling boil. Add the pasta and stir once. Cook until al dente (firm to the bite) according to the package directions. Drain and return the pasta to the pot in which it was cooked, then add the sauce.

6. Mix together to distribute the sauce evenly through the pasta. Transfer to a warmed serving dish or individual pasta bowls to serve at once.

PASTA TIP
If you are a little squeamish, ask your fishmonger to prepare the monkfish and sardines for you.

SPAGHETTI WITH ORANGE

Here is a very light and delicious pasta dish with fresh orange and mint. Perfect for hot summer days, it makes a good lunch dish with a green salad.

SERVES 4

400g spaghetti
4 tablespoons olive oil
8 anchovy fillets preserved in oil, drained and chopped
Zest and juice of ½ orange (thinly slice the zest into strips, avoiding the pith)
4 tablespoons dried breadcrumbs
20 peeled orange segments
1 small handful of mint leaves, rinsed and roughly chopped, to garnish

1. Bring a large saucepan of salted water to a rolling boil. Add the spaghetti and cook according to the package directions until al dente (firm to the bite).

2. Meanwhile, heat the oil in a large frying pan and gently fry the anchovies until they melt into the oil.

3. Remove the pan from the heat and stir in the orange zest and juice, dried breadcrumbs and the orange segments.

4. Drain the cooked spaghetti and add to the frying pan. Sauté over medium heat for 2–3 minutes. Transfer to a warmed serving dish, scatter with chopped mint and serve at once.

PASTA WITH BREADCRUMBS

This is a very old-fashioned pasta dish, which, like other dishes from the south, uses breadcrumbs toasted in oil in place of grated cheese.

SERVES 4

6 salted anchovy fillets
10 tablespoons olive oil
5 tablespoons very hard, dry coarse breadcrumbs
400g bucatini or spaghetti
2 tablespoons finely chopped flat leaf parsley, to garnish

1. Rinse and bone the anchovy fillets, then chop into small pieces. Place in a large frying pan with the oil. Melt the anchovy into the oil over medium heat.

2. After 2 or 3 minutes sprinkle in the breadcrumbs. Toast until golden brown, then remove from the heat and set aside until needed.

3. Bring a large saucepan of salted water to a rolling boil. Add the pasta and cook until al dente (firm to the bite), then drain and add to the pan with the breadcrumbs, anchovies and oil. Quickly mix together over medium heat to warm through.

4. Transfer to a warm serving dish or individual pasta bowls. Sprinkle with chopped parsley and serve at once.

FETTUCCINE WITH PRAWNS & ARTICHOKES

SERVES 4

3 fresh globe artichokes

A little lemon juice

6 tablespoons extra virgin olive oil

2 garlic cloves, peeled and finely
  chopped

3 tablespoons finely chopped flat
  leaf parsley

20 medium-sized raw shelled prawns

$\frac{1}{2}$ glass of dry white wine or
  fish stock

350g fettuccine

Sea salt and freshly ground
  black pepper

1. First, trim the artichokes, removing all the hard outer leaves and the choke. Drop them into a basin of cold water with a little lemon juice to prevent discoloration.

2. Boil the artichoke hearts in salted water for about 10 minutes until tender. When they are ready, drain and pat dry. Thinly slice into strips.

3. Bring a large pot of salted water to a rolling boil.

4. Meanwhile, heat half the oil in a pan with half the garlic and add the sliced artichokes. Stir and season, sprinkle with half the parsley and fry together until cooked through and slightly crispy. Set aside.

5. Slice the prawns in half lengthways, remove the black strip of the gut and rinse and dry thoroughly.

6. Fry the rest of the garlic in the remaining oil until just pungent, then add the clean prawns and sauté together for 3 or 4 minutes, basting with the white wine or stock. Season and set aside, but keep warm.

7. Cook the fettuccine in the boiling salted water until al dente (firm to the bite) according to the package directions. Return to the pot in which it was cooked, or a large, wide frying pan.

8. Add the artichokes and the prawns, heat and mix together thoroughly.

9. Transfer to a warmed serving platter, scatter with the rest of the parsley and serve at once.

BLACK INK PASTA WITH SCALLOPS & LIME

Personally, I am not very fond of coloured pasta, although I do think the green spinach or the black cuttlefish ink varieties can look very dramatic and actually can taste rather good, when appropriately dressed with the right sauce.

SERVES 6

Extra virgin olive oil
10 fresh scallops, cleaned and corals removed (your fishmonger can do this for you)
2 fresh limes, rinsed and dried
400g black cuttlefish ink pasta such as tagliatelle or bavette
1 large handful of flat leaf parsley, chopped, to garnish
Sea salt and freshly ground black pepper

1. Heat a pan until piping hot. Brush with a little olive oil and quickly sear the scallops on either side for 2 minutes.

2. Zest the limes and squeeze the juice from them.

3. Bring a large pot of salted water to a rolling boil, toss in the pasta and stir once. Cook until al dente (firm to the bite) according to the package directions and then drain thoroughly. Return the pasta to the hot pot.

4. Add the scallops, zest and juice of the limes and about 4 tablespoons olive oil. Season to taste with salt and pepper.

5. Return to the heat and turn the mixture quickly for about 1 minute to heat through. If liked, add the corals and cook until just opaque. Transfer to a warm serving dish and sprinkle with parsley just before serving.

MUSSELS CARBONARA

Beaten egg yolks are used to draw this fishy pasta dish together, which, along with lots of freshly ground black pepper, are the characteristics that give it the name 'carbonara'.

SERVES 4

1kg fresh mussels, cleaned and scrubbed in several changes of fresh water and beards removed
4 tablespoons extra virgin olive oil
1 medium-sized onion, peeled and thinly sliced
1 garlic clove, lightly crushed
350g spaghetti
4 egg yolks, beaten
1 small handful of flat leaf parsley, finely chopped
Sea salt and freshly ground black pepper

1. Place the mussels in a wide frying pan, covered, over a fairly high heat and shake the pan frequently to help the mussels open up. After about 6 minutes, they should all be open. Note: Any mussels that have not opened up after this time should be discarded. Unopened shellfish can make you ill.

2. Remove the mussels from the open shells and set aside, carefully wiping away any trace of sand or sediment. Discard the shells and reserve the cooking liquid, strained.

3. Heat the olive oil in a separate pan and fry the onion and garlic together until softened, then add the shelled mussels and the strained cooking liquid.

4. Meanwhile, bring a large pot of salted water to a rolling boil, add the pasta and cook until al dente (firm to the bite) according to the package directions. Drain and tip into the pan with the mussels.

5. Mix together, adding the egg yolks, parsley and plenty of freshly ground black pepper.

6. As soon as the eggs have lightly scrambled, transfer the pasta to a warmed serving dish or individual pasta bowls and serve at once.

ZITI WITH FRESH TUNA & BLACK OLIVES

Make sure you choose really tasty black olives from which you remove the stones yourself to ensure a lovely tangy olive flavour in this dish.

SERVES 4

2 medium-sized fresh tuna steaks
5 tablespoons extra virgin olive oil
1 garlic clove
½ glass of dry white wine
4 ripe tomatoes, roughly chopped
12 black olives, pitted
400g ziti, or another thick, tubular
    pasta such as maccheroni or penne
1 tablespoon dried oregano, to
    garnish
Sea salt and freshly ground
    black pepper

1. Cut the tuna steaks into small cubes.

2. Heat the oil in a pan and fry the garlic until it turns brown. Discard and add the tuna.

3. Fry the tuna quickly on both sides for 3–4 minutes each side. Pour in the white wine and allow the alcohol to evaporate (about 2 minutes).

4. Add the tomatoes and the olives, stir and season with salt and pepper. Keep warm over a gentle heat.

5. Meanwhile, bring a large pot of salted water to a rolling boil. Add the pasta and stir once. Cook until al dente (firm to the bite) according to the package directions.

6. Drain the pasta and return it to the pot in which it was cooked. Add the tuna sauce and stir together.

7. Transfer to a warmed serving dish or individual pasta bowls. Sprinkle with dried oregano and serve at once.

RIGATONI WITH ANCHOVIES & AUBERGINES

SERVES 4

2 long aubergines
300ml extra virgin olive oil
6 salted anchovies, boned and
    washed thoroughly, then dried
1 tablespoon caster sugar
1 dessertspoon fine salt
2 garlic cloves, peeled and halved
1 teaspoon crushed, dried chilli
    pepper
600g canned tomatoes, drained and
    chopped
2 heaped tablespoons finely chopped
    flat leaf parsley
400g rigatoni
Sea salt

1. Slice the aubergines in half lengthways and put them in a large pan. Cover with olive oil (reserve about 3 tablespoons) and set over a very low heat for about 1 hour until soft and slightly caramelized, turning every so often. Drain thoroughly, cool and remove all the flesh. Set aside.

2. Divide the boned anchovies in two and cover one half with sugar and fine salt. Leave to stand for about 10 minutes, then rinse and mix with the aubergines.

3. Heat the remaining olive oil in a pan with the garlic and chilli until the garlic is just browned. Discard the garlic and add the remaining anchovies. Stir until the anchovies dissolve.

4. Stir in the canned tomatoes and season with salt. Leave to simmer for about 20 minutes, then stir in half the chopped parsley. Set aside, but keep warm.

5. Bring a large pot of salted water to a rolling boil. Add the pasta and cook until al dente (firm to the bite) according to the package directions. Drain and return to the same pot in which it was cooked.

6. Add the sauce and the aubergine pulp. Mix together thoroughly and transfer to a warmed serving dish or individual pasta bowls with a final sprinkling of chopped parsley.

CELLENTANI WITH SAFFRON

SERVES 4

4–5 tablespoons extra virgin olive oil
1 large spring onion, trimmed and
   chopped
6 baby courgettes, rinsed and thinly
   sliced
6 tablespoons fresh or frozen peas
10g saffron powder, diluted with
   ½ ladleful boiling water
400g fresh mussels, cleaned and
   scrubbed in several changes of
   fresh water and beards removed
1 glass of dry white wine
400g cellentani
12 cherry tomatoes, chopped
200g cooked shelled prawns
½ teaspoon dried crushed chillies
Sea salt and freshly ground
   black pepper

1. Heat 2 tablespoons of the olive oil in a large frying pan and fry the spring onion until soft.

2. Add the sliced courgettes and the peas and stir together. Cook until softened, about 10 minutes, and then add the diluted saffron. Season and continue to cook for about 10 minutes.

3. Put the cleaned mussels into a separate pan with the wine. Cover and place over a medium heat, shaking the pan occasionally to encourage the mussels to open up. After 8 minutes, all the mussels should have opened. Note: Any that remain closed should be discarded.

4. Drain the mussels and reserve the cooking liquid. Remove and discard the shells. Set the shelled mussels and their liquid aside until required, keeping the liquid warm.

5. Bring a large pot of salted water to a rolling boil. Add the pasta and stir once. Cook according to the package directions until al dente (firm to the bite), then drain and return to the pot in which it was cooked. Add 1 tablespoon of the remaining olive oil and toss together.

6. Add the spring onion, courgette and pea mixture, the mussels and their cooking liquid, cherry tomatoes, cooked prawns and crushed chillies to the pot. Mix everything together and serve at once, dressed with any remaining olive oil.

SALMON-FILLED TORTELLONI

This is a very time-consuming dish to make, but it is nevertheless fun and the results are so fantastic that it is really worth the effort. Take your time and do be sure the pasta parcels are well sealed so as not to lose any of the wonderful filling.

SERVES 10 (ABOUT 8 TORTELLONI PER PERSON)

200g flaked hot smoked salmon and flaked cooked fresh salmon, mixed together
200g smoked salmon, finely chopped
100g fresh ricotta cheese, mashed with a little milk
2 egg yolks
2 tablespoons finely chopped flat leaf parsley
Sea salt and freshly ground black pepper

PASTA
350g plain white pasta flour, 00, plus extra for rolling out
350g fine semolina
7 eggs

1. To make the filling, combine the salmon with the ricotta in a large bowl.

2. Stir in the egg yolks, parsley and seasoning. Set aside while you make the pasta dough.

3. To make the tortelloni, pile the flour and semolina on a work surface and follow the instructions to make fresh pasta on page 20, steps 1–3.

4. On a floured surface, roll out the dough as thinly as possible with a strong long rolling pin. Continue to roll it over and over again until really elastic, smooth and shiny. When it is ready, the sheet of dough will feel exactly like a brand new, wrung-out, damp chamois.

5. If you use a pasta machine, after resting the dough break off a piece about the size of a small fist (always re-wrap the pasta you are not using). Flatten slightly with your hands and push through the widest setting on your machine. Fold in half and repeat. Do this until an air pocket forms in the fold and you can hear a small pop as the pasta comes through the gap.

SAUCE

³⁄₄ litre double cream

4 thin sheets of smoked salmon,
   cut into thin strips

3 tablespoons chopped flat leaf
   parsley

6. Move the machine down to the next setting and put the pasta through twice. Continue in this way, changing the setting after the second time the pasta has gone through the rollers, right to the last (or penultimate) setting on the machine, depending on how fine you want it to be.

7. Lay the sheet of pasta carefully on to a very lightly floured surface and proceed to fill the dough immediately, covering the rolled out pasta with a slightly damp clean tea towel to prevent it drying out as you work (see Filling & Shaping Tortelloni, page 23).

8. Bring a saucepan of salted water to a rolling boil and cook the tortelloni until al dente (firm to the bite), about 5–7 minutes.

9. Meanwhile, warm the cream gently in a pan without allowing it to boil too hard.

10. Drain the pasta and return to the pot, pour over the cream and toss together gently.

11. Arrange in a warmed serving dish, sprinkle with smoked salmon strips and parsley, then serve at once.

PASTA TIP

When filling the tortelloni, work quickly to prevent the pasta from drying out too much. It is almost impossible to fill and seal pasta that is dry. A tiny smear of cold water or egg white around the edges will help to seal the edges, but bending it into shape can soon become too difficult.

LINGUINE WITH CREAMY PRAWN SAUCE

The long, flat spaghetti, linguine, works very well in this delicately flavoured dish. Perfect as a starter, or as a single dish with a big bowl of salad.

SERVES 4

3 tablespoons unsalted butter

1 small onion, peeled and finely chopped

1 small leek or shallot, very finely chopped

250g small raw prawns

4 tablespoons dry white wine

400g linguine

7 tablespoons single or double cream

2 tablespoons chopped flat leaf parsley

Sea salt and freshly ground black pepper

1. Bring a large saucepan of salted water to a rolling boil.

2. Meanwhile, heat the butter in a pan and fry the onion and chopped leek or shallot together for a few minutes or until soft.

3. Add the prawns and stir together well. Cook for 5 minutes, then add the wine and boil off the alcohol, about 2 minutes. Season with salt and pepper and take off the heat.

4. Cook the pasta in the boiling water until al dente (firm to the bite) according to the package directions. Drain thoroughly and return to the same pot. Keep warm.

5. Pour the cream over the prawns and return to the heat. Stir and heat through for about 1 minute, season well and then pour the sauce over the cooked pasta.

6. Toss together, add the parsley and toss again to thoroughly combine the pasta and sauce. Transfer to a warmed serving bowl or individual plates and serve at once.

SPAGHETTI WITH CLAMS & TOMATO

SERVES 4

1kg fresh Venus clams (vongole),
  cleaned and scrubbed in several
  changes of fresh water
4 tablespoons dry white wine
4 tablespoons extra virgin olive oil
2 garlic cloves, peeled and finely
  chopped
400g passata (sieved tomatoes)
3 tablespoons chopped flat leaf
  parsley
400g spaghetti or vermicelli
Sea salt and freshly ground
  black pepper

1. Clean the clams really thoroughly in several changes of fresh water to ensure all traces of sand or mud are removed to avoid a gritty taste. When the water from the clams is completely clear, they are clean.

2. Transfer to a wide, fairly deep, frying pan with the wine. Cover and heat the pan. When the pan is hot, shake frequently to help turn the clams so they will open up – any that have not opened up after about 6 or 7 minutes must be discarded.

3. Drain and reserve the cooking liquid. Remove the clams from their shells. Discard most of the shells, reserving a few for garnish.

4. Heat the oil and add the garlic. Stir and then fry for about 5 minutes until golden. Add the passata.

5. Strain in the reserved cooking liquid and season. Simmer for about 15 minutes or until the sauce reduces by about one-third.

6. Add the clams and parsley, stir and heat through. Take off the heat.

7. While the sauce reduces, bring a large pot of salted water to a rolling boil. Add the pasta and stir once. Cover and return to the boil. Remove the lid and boil until al dente (firm to the bite) according to the package directions. Drain and return to the pot.

8. Pour over the sauce, toss together thoroughly and transfer to a warmed platter to serve.

SPAGHETTI WITH COURGETTES & MUSSELS

SERVES 4

4 tender courgettes, skins shaven into strips and flesh cut into small cubes

5 tablespoons extra virgin olive oil

600g fresh mussels, cleaned and scrubbed in several changes of fresh water and beards removed

2 garlic cloves, peeled and lightly crushed

20 cherry tomatoes, rinsed and halved

2 tablespoons unsalted butter

400g spaghetti

2 tablespoons finely chopped flat leaf parsley

Sea salt and freshly ground black pepper

1. Blanch the courgette skins in boiling water for 1 minute. Drain with a slotted spoon, then plunge into a bowl of iced water to retain their colour and texture. Set aside until required.

2. Heat a small amount of the oil in a pan and fry the courgette flesh until just softened, then set aside.

3. Put the mussels into a pan set over a medium heat and cover. Shake the pan occasionally to open up the mussels, then drain. Any that remain closed must be discarded. Strain the cooking liquid into a bowl. Shell the mussels and add to the liquid. Set aside.

4. Fry the garlic in the remaining oil until pungent. Add the shelled mussels and half their liquid, stir and season.

5. Cook the garlic and mussels together for a few minutes, then add the tomatoes. Stir again and cook for a further 8 minutes. Take off the heat, discard the garlic and add the courgette cubes. Stir and adjust the seasoning, then set aside.

6. Melt the butter in a small pan. Add the drained strips of courgette skin and fry for about 5 minutes. Season and set aside.

7. Bring a large saucepan of salted water and the remaining mussel liquid to a rolling boil and cook the spaghetti until al dente (firm to the bite) according to the package directions. Drain and return to the saucepan. Add the mussel and courgette sauce, the fried courgette skins and parsley. Mix together and transfer to a warmed platter to serve at once.

LINGUINE WITH SQUID

This is a slightly spicy sauce, tempered by the sweetness of the squid. Make sure the squid has long enough to cook until really tender.

SERVES 4

500g fresh tomatoes
3 garlic cloves, peeled and chopped
8 tablespoons extra virgin olive oil
1 teaspoon concentrated tomato
  purée
4 small fresh squid, cleaned and
  sliced
1 glass of dry white wine
2 small dried red chillies, finely
  chopped
350g linguine
3 tablespoons chopped flat leaf
  parsley, to garnish
Sea salt

1. Drop the tomatoes into boiling water for 1 minute, then peel and roughly chop.

2. In a saucepan, heat together the garlic and oil until sizzling. Add the tomatoes and the tomato purée. Stir together for a few minutes and then add the squid and seal for 1 minute.

3. Add the wine and allow the alcohol to evaporate, about 2 minutes, before lowering the heat to a low simmer. Sprinkle with salt and chopped chillies. Cover and simmer slowly for about 1 hour or until the squid is very soft.

4. Meanwhile, bring a saucepan of salted water to a rolling boil. Cook the linguine until al dente (firm to the bite) according to the package directions. Drain and toss with the sauce. Scatter with chopped parsley and serve at once.

PASTA, MUSSELS & BEANS

Any short, smallish pasta shape works well in this elegant dish. Pasta, mussels and beans make a fantastic combination.

SERVES 4

½ kg fresh mussels, cleaned and scrubbed in several changes of fresh water and beards removed
1 garlic clove, peeled and lightly crushed
1 small handful of flat leaf parsley, half of it finely chopped
4 tablespoons extra virgin olive oil
200g penne or other short pasta
200g canned cannellini or borlotti beans, drained
6 tablespoons single cream
Sea salt and freshly ground black pepper

1. Put the mussels in a large saucepan with the garlic and the parsley that has not been chopped. Cover with a lid, place over a medium heat and shake the pan occasionally to open up the mussels, about 8 minutes. Note: any mussels that have not opened after this time should be discarded immediately.

2. Tip the mussels into a large, shallow pan that is large enough to hold the pasta, too. Add the olive oil and season with salt and pepper. Set aside.

3. Meanwhile, bring a large saucepan of salted water to a rolling boil. Cook the pasta according to the package directions until al dente (firm to the bite).

4. While the pasta is cooking, mash the beans with the cream and some of the strained liquid from the mussels to make a thick purée. Gently warm through.

5. Once the pasta is cooked, drain and transfer to the pan with the mussels. Heat briefly over a low heat, combining the pasta and mussels.

6. Divide the warm bean purée between 4 warmed pasta bowls. Tip the pasta evenly over the top, sprinkle with the chopped parsley and serve.

FISH & PRAWN-FILLED PASTA ROLL

A fresh interpretation of a pasta dish, it looks very different yet tastes delicious. It can be made well in advance, frozen in its cloth, and can wait in the hot cooking water for up to 30 minutes without mishap.

SERVES 6

400g cooked white fish
150g cooked shelled prawns, coarsely chopped
2 tablespoons freshly chopped flat leaf parsley
½ teaspoon grated lemon zest, plus 1 teaspoon lemon juice
9–12 tablespoons cold thin Béchamel sauce, (see pages 34–5), made using some of the stock from the fish or prawns
Tomato sauce (see page 177) or melted butter, to serve
Sea salt and freshly ground black pepper

PASTA

500g plain white pasta flour, 00, plus extra for rolling out
5 eggs
A pinch of sea salt

1. Stir the fish, prawns, parsley, lemon zest and juice and Béchamel sauce together for the filling. Season to taste and then set aside until required.

2. Make the fresh pasta as usual (see pages 19–20) and roll out on a floured surface into a wide sheet by hand. The pasta sheet should be slightly smaller than the muslin cloth in which it will be wrapped – about 23 x 35 cm. Spread filling over the top (keep within 3cm of the edges) and then roll up from the shorter edge like a Swiss roll, making sure there is no air between each turn of the spiral.

3. Wrap tightly in a clean muslin and be sure to tie the ends tightly.

4. Bring a fish kettle of salted water to the boil. Slide the wrapped roll carefully into the water and gently boil for about 1 hour to cook through. Do not let the roll sag in the centre!

5. Carefully remove the roll and drain on kitchen paper or a tea towel. Unwrap and lay on a board to quickly slice with a sharp knife.

6. Arrange the slices on a warmed serving plate and spoon over a little tomato sauce or melted butter to serve.

SPAGHETTI WITH CLAMS

As with all recipes using clams (vongole), make sure they are as clean as possible before you cook them to avoid an unpleasant muddy taste or a gritty sensation under your teeth. Rinse in several changes of water until the water runs clear.

SERVES 4

1½ kg fresh baby Venus clams (vongole), cleaned and scrubbed in several changes of fresh water
6 tablespoons extra virgin olive oil
3 garlic cloves, peeled and finely chopped
400g spaghetti or vermicelli
3 tablespoons chopped flat leaf parsley
Sea salt and freshly ground black pepper

1. Place the cleaned clams in a wide, fairly deep frying pan with about 2 tablespoons of the oil. Cover and heat.

2. When the pan is very hot, shake it regularly over the heat to help the clams open up.

3. After about 6–7 minutes the clams that are going to open will have done so. Discard any that remain closed immediately, drain the rest and reserve the cooking liquid.

4. Heat the remaining oil with the garlic for a few minutes, then add the clams and strain over the reserved liquid.

5. Mix everything together and bring to the boil, then cover and take off the heat. Keep warm.

6. Meanwhile, bring a large saucepan of salted water to a rolling boil. Add the pasta and stir once. Cover, return to the boil and then boil, uncovered, until al dente (firm to the bite) according to the package directions. Drain and return to the saucepan.

7. Pour over the clams and toss everything together. Add the parsley and plenty of freshly ground black pepper. Toss again and transfer to a warmed platter or bowl. Serve at once.

TAGLIATELLE WITH MUSSELS

It is essential that you clean and wash all the fresh mussels very carefully before cooking and any that have not opened up after the cooking time must not be forced open.

SERVES 4–6

500g fresh mussels, cleaned and
   scrubbed in several changes of
   fresh water and beards removed
350g tagliatelle
4 tablespoons olive oil
2 garlic cloves, finely chopped
3 tablespoons chopped parsley
400g chopped and deseeded fresh
   ripe tomatoes
Sea salt and freshly ground
   black pepper

1. Place the cleaned mussels in a wide frying pan, covered, over a fairly high heat, shaking the pan frequently to help them open up. After about 6 minutes, they should all be open. Note: Any mussels that have not opened up after this time should be discarded.

2. Remove the cooked mussels from the open shells and set aside, carefully wiping away any trace of sand or sediment. Discard the shells.

3. Bring a large pot of salted water to a rolling boil and toss in the pasta. Stir once and return to the boil. Cook until al dente (firm to the bite) according to the package directions.

4. Meanwhile, heat the oil in a large frying pan with the garlic and parsley. Fry for 5 minutes, then add the tomatoes. Season and stir, then cook over a high heat for about 10 minutes. Stir in the shelled mussels, heat through for 2 or 3 minutes and then remove from the heat.

5. When the pasta is cooked, drain carefully and return to the pot in which it was cooked. Pour over the sauce and stir to combine. Transfer to warmed pasta bowls and serve at once.

PASTA SALAD WITH SALMON

This very modern, elegant pasta salad uses thinly sliced raw salmon marinated in lemon juice, oil and fresh tarragon to make a really delicious summer dish.

SERVES 6

3 tablespoons finely chopped
   tarragon
1 dried red chilli pepper
3 tablespoons lemon juice
5 tablespoons extra virgin olive oil
3 medium-sized fresh salmon steaks,
   skinned
500g fusilli
Sea salt and freshly ground
   black pepper

1. Put the tarragon, chilli pepper, lemon juice, olive oil and salt and pepper to taste in a small bowl. Whisk together and set aside until needed.

2. Slice the salmon as thinly as possible into fine strips.

3. Remove the chilli and pour the prepared dressing over the salmon strips. Leave to marinate for 1 hour at room temperature, stirring occasionally to coat in the marinade.

4. Meanwhile, bring a large pot of salted water to a rolling boil. Add the fusilli and cook until al dente (firm to the bite) according to the package instructions. Drain and tip into a large serving bowl.

5. Pour the marinated salmon mixture over the top and mix together to distribute the salmon evenly through the pasta.

6. Leave to stand (or chill in the refrigerator) for about 1 hour, then mix once more before serving.

CHEESE
& EGG

BUCATINI ALLA SICILIANA

Taleggio is a deliciously creamy, soft cheese from northern Italy, but any similar kind of cheese will also work well in this recipe. Try Camembert or Brie, for example.

SERVES 4

6 ripe cherry tomatoes
1 aubergine, rinsed
12 black olives, pitted
4 large tablespoons extra virgin olive oil, plus extra for greasing
1 handful of basil leaves, rinsed and shredded
400g bucatini
100g taleggio, diced
Sea salt and freshly ground black pepper

PASTA TIP
Blanching allows you to easily remove the tomato skins. Simply make a small slash in the skin, place in a bowl and cover with boiling water. Leave to stand for 2 minutes, then remove with a slotted spoon and slip off the skins.

1. Preheat the oven to 190°C/375°F/Gas Mark 5.

2. Meanwhile, blanch the tomatoes in boiling water for 2 minutes (see tip). Remove from the water with a slotted spoon, then peel, deseed and dice.

3. Slice the aubergine and the olives into small dice and transfer to a sieve. Leave to drain over a bowl for about 30 minutes.

4. Heat the olive oil in a shallow pan and fry together the tomatoes, aubergines, olives and basil for about 10 minutes to soften them.

5. Meanwhile, bring a large saucepan of salted water to a rolling boil and then add the bucatini. Cook, stirring frequently to prevent the pasta from sticking together, until al dente (firm to the bite) according to the package directions.

6. Drain and transfer to a bowl. Add the tomato, aubergine and olive mixture, season and stir to thoroughly combine.

7. Grease an ovenproof dish large enough to hold the pasta mixture (about 20cm diameter) and then arrange the dressed bucatini inside.

8. Scatter with taleggio and bake in the oven for about 10 minutes, or until the cheese has melted and then serve at once.

FETTUCCINE WITH SUN-DRIED TOMATOES

In this recipe the almost chocolate flavour of the sun-dried tomatoes combines with deliciously fresh ricotta as a background, and then a little pesto for extra piquancy.

SERVES 4

350g fettuccine

4 heaped tablespoons fresh ricotta cheese

1$\frac{1}{2}$ tablespoons freshly grated Parmesan or pecorino cheese

2 tablespoons good-quality Pesto (see page 67)

2 tablespoons olive oil

8–12 sun-dried tomatoes preserved in oil, drained with oil reserved, cut into thin strips

Sea salt and freshly ground black pepper

1. Bring a large saucepan of salted water to a rolling boil. Toss in the pasta, stir well, cover and return to the boil. Remove the lid and boil for about 2 minutes or according to the package directions until al dente (firm to the bite), stirring frequently.

2. Meanwhile, mash the cheeses together.

3. Drain the pasta, but not too thoroughly. Return it to the warm cooking saucepan. Add the mixed cheese and toss together well.

4. Stir in the pesto, the olive oil and half the sun-dried tomatoes with their oil. Mix together thoroughly. Add a little salt and pepper at this stage, if required.

5. Transfer to a warmed bowl, sprinkle with the remaining strips of sun-dried tomato and serve at once.

CREAMY PASTA WITH HAM

A very delicate, soothing sort of pasta dish – which makes great comfort food! For extra flavour, add a little freshly ground black pepper or finely chopped fresh herbs such as parsley, basil, thyme or sage.

SERVES 4

400g conchiglie
50g unsalted butter
100g mascarpone cheese
100g ricotta cheese
50g thick-cut cooked ham, sliced
   into matchstick strips
Sea salt

1. Bring a large saucepan of salted water to a rolling boil, add the pasta and stir once. Cook until al dente (firm to the bite) according to the package directions.

2. While the pasta is cooking, mash together the butter, mascarpone and ricotta. Use a little of the boiling water to smooth out any lumps.

3. Mix together the creamy mixture and the strips of ham.

4. Drain the pasta and return it to the saucepan in which it was cooked. Toss everything together thoroughly and serve at once.

RIGATONI WITH FONTINA

Fontina is a deliciously buttery cow's milk cheese with a wonderfully nutty flavour that is made exclusively in the tiny region of Val d'Aosta.

SERVES 4

400g rigatoni
2½ tablespoons unsalted butter
200g pancetta, diced
300g fontina cheese, diced
6 tablespoons double cream
Sea salt and freshly ground
   black pepper

1. Bring a large saucepan of salted water to a rolling boil and cook the rigatoni until al dente (firm to the bite) according to the package directions.

2. Meanwhile, melt the butter in a pan and fry the pancetta until crispy, about 10 minutes. Set aside.

3. Drain the rigatoni and return to the warm cooking saucepan, then add the pancetta, fontina and cream. Mix together thoroughly until the cheese melts.

4. Add some freshly milled black pepper and serve at once.

FUSILLI WITH CHEESE FONDUE, WALNUTS & TRUFFLES

SERVES 4

½ tablespoon unsalted butter
1 tablespoon plain white flour
½ litre milk
100g taleggio cheese, diced
100g fontina cheese, diced
4 tablespoons freshly grated
   Parmesan cheese
2 tablespoons shelled walnuts,
   chopped
1 free-range egg yolk
300g fusilli
1 small fresh truffle, shaved, or
   1 dessertspoon truffles preserved
   in oil or truffle butter
1 tablespoon chopped flat leaf
   parsley, to garnish.
Sea salt and freshly ground
   black pepper

1. Melt the butter in a saucepan until foaming. Stir in the flour to make a smooth paste (roux). Add the milk and stir again. Simmer until the sauce has thickened and then season with salt and pepper to taste.

2. Add the cheeses, walnuts and egg yolk (see tip). Stir until well blended and keep warm.

3. Bring a large saucepan of salted water to a rolling boil and cook the fusilli until al dente (firm to the bite) according to the package directions. Drain and then return to the warm cooking saucepan.

4. Pour over the sauce and mix together thoroughly to combine (add a few spoonfuls of the pasta cooking water, if necessary, to help slake the sauce).

5. Transfer to a warmed serving dish and scatter the fresh or preserved truffle over the top. Sprinkle with parsley and serve at once.

PASTA TIP
If using truffle butter, melt into the sauce with the cheeses and use sparingly as it can be intensely flavoured.

PASTA CARBONARA

This is a hugely popular classic sauce for pasta, traditionally served with bucatini or spaghetti. In the original recipe, no cream is added to the dish.

SERVES 4

400g bucatini or spaghetti
200g pancetta, guanciale (see tip) or
   best-quality streaky bacon, diced
3 eggs, beaten
5 tablespoons grated pecorino or
   Parmesan cheese, plus extra
   to serve
Sea salt and freshly ground
   black pepper

1. Bring a large saucepan of salted water to a rolling boil. Add the pasta and stir well. Replace the lid and return to the boil. Remove or adjust the lid once the water is boiling again. Cook according to the package directions until al dente (firm to the bite).

2. While the pasta is cooking, fry the pancetta in a very hot frying pan until crisp and the fat runs freely.

3. Meanwhile, beat the eggs in a bowl with the cheese and plenty of black pepper. When the pasta is cooked, drain and return to the saucepan.

4. Pour over the eggs, cheese and pancetta and quickly stir all the ingredients together so that the eggs lightly scramble and pull the dish together. The fat from the pancetta will sizzle and fry as it mingles with the pasta. Serve at once sprinkled with extra parmesan and freshly ground black pepper, if liked.

PASTA TIP
Guanciale is bacon taken from the jowl of a pig and considered by many to be better than bacon made from the belly.

CANNELLONI WITH RADICCHIO

SERVES 6

100g unsalted butter, plus extra
   for greasing
55g plain white flour
$\frac{1}{2}$ litre milk
1kg radicchio, rinsed, trimmed and
   hard stems removed
3 tablespoons extra virgin olive oil
1 garlic clove
350g lasagna
200g Emmenthal cheese, diced
150g chopped ham
6 tablespoons freshly grated
   Parmesan cheese
Sea salt and freshly ground
   black pepper

1. Preheat the oven to 180°C/350°F/Gas Mark 4. Meanwhile, melt half the butter in a saucepan until foaming, then add the flour and mix together until well blended.

2. Add the milk and whisk until smooth. Gently cook the sauce for about 15 minutes or until thickened and smooth, then season with salt.

3. Boil the radicchio in salted water for about 5 minutes, then drain and coarsely chop.

4. Heat the oil in a pan with half the remaining butter and the garlic clove until the garlic is golden brown. Discard the garlic and add the radicchio. Stir together, season and cook for a further 20 minutes until the radicchio is wilted, stirring frequently.

5. Meanwhile, bring a large saucepan of salted water to a rolling boil and blanch the fresh lasagna sheets in small batches for 1 minute, then remove with a slotted spoon. Refresh the lasagna in a tray of cold water. Leave to one side, covered with cold water to prevent from sticking together.

6. When the lasagna is blanched, lay each sheet on a board and fill with a little white sauce, a little radicchio, a little cheese and ham. Add a sprinkling of Parmesan and roll up into a cannelloni.

7. Butter an ovenproof dish, about 20cm square, and arrange the filled cannelloni inside, side by side. Cover with the remaining white sauce and Parmesan. Bake for 30 minutes and then serve straight from the dish.

FUSILLI WITH CREAM, PECORINO & PARMESAN

This is another, very simple and comforting pasta dish with an interesting contrast between sharp pecorino and the buttery Parmesan, tempered by the cream.

SERVES 6

500g fusilli
30ml milk
4 tablespoons single cream
$\frac{1}{4}$ teaspoon dried chilli pepper
3 tablespoons extra virgin olive oil
3 tablespoons freshly grated pecorino
  cheese
3 tablespoons freshly grated
  Parmesan cheese
Sea salt

1. Bring a large saucepan of salted water to a rolling boil and cook the fusilli according to the package directions until al dente (firm to the bite).
2. Meanwhile, warm the milk and cream together in a saucepan. Add the chilli and season with salt.
3. Drain the pasta and return to the warm cooking saucepan. Pour over the sauce and mix together well. Add the oil and cheeses, reserving a little Parmesan for sprinkling.
4. Transfer to a warmed serving dish or individual bowls and sprinkle with the remaining Parmesan just before serving.

SPAGHETTI FRITTATA

You could use any kind of leftover pasta for this dish, but spaghetti looks quite pretty. Add in leftover scraps of cheese, grated, some cooked vegetables – and anything else you think might work as a frittata.

SERVES 4–6

Between 1 and 4 servings of leftover spaghetti with tomato or other vegetable sauce
6 eggs, beaten
2 tablespoons freshly grated Parmesan cheese
4 tablespoons olive oil
Sea salt and freshly ground black pepper

1. Mix the cold pasta into the beaten eggs. Add the Parmesan and seasoning, then mix together well.

2. Heat the oil in a wide, shallow pan. When it is very hot, pour in the egg mixture. Shake the pan to flatten and even out the mixture, pulling the liquid egg into the centre as you work.

3. Cook until the underside is browned and firm, about 5–10 minutes depending on the thickness of your pan. Turn over the frittata by covering the pan with a large, flat lid or plate and overturn the pan onto it. Return the pan to the heat and carefully slide the frittata (uncooked side underneath) back into the hot pan. Continue cooking until golden brown and firm on the underside, between 3–8 minutes.

4. Slide the frittata out onto a clean, flat platter and serve hot or cold.

RICOTTA-FILLED RAVIOLI

SERVES 6 (ABOUT 7 RAVIOLI PER PERSON)

400g ricotta cheese
A pinch of grated nutmeg
175g freshly grated Parmesan cheese
1 egg
$\frac{1}{4}$ teaspoon olive oil
150g unsalted butter
5 sage leaves (rub gently between
   your palms to release their flavour)
Sea salt and freshly ground
   black pepper
PASTA
250g plain white pasta flour, 00,
   plus extra for rolling out
250g fine semolina
5 eggs

1. To make the filling, mash the ricotta in a bowl. Add the nutmeg, seasoning and half the Parmesan. Blend together with 1 egg and set aside until needed.

2. For the pasta, tip the flour and semolina out onto a work surface and follow the instructions to make fresh pasta on pages 19–20.

3. Unwrap the dough and roll out onto a floured surface several times until fine and silky. Divide lengthways into 6cm wide strips.

4. Drop $\frac{1}{2}$ dessertspoon filling along the length of each strip, leaving a 2-cm border. Fold in half to enclose the filling.

5. Using a pastry cutter or an upturned glass, cut around each section of filling to make a crescent. Seal the curved edge with the prongs of a fork. Continue in this way until all the dough has been cut.

6. Bring a large saucepan of salted water to a rolling boil. Drop the ravioli into the water and boil until floating on the surface and tender. While the pasta is cooking, gently melt the oil and butter with the sage leaves until warm and golden, not browned.

7. Drain the cooking water for the pasta carefully, remove with a slotted spoon and arrange the ravioli in a warmed serving dish. Pour the sage sauce on top and mix carefully to distribute. Sprinkle with the rest of the cheese and serve at once

PASTA TIP
Any remaining scraps of dough can be finely chopped with a sharp knife and set aside to dry. Add to a clear broth to make a simple soup.

GARGANELLI WITH AUBERGINES & RICOTTA

A speciality from Bologna, garganelli are a handmade penne made with egg pasta, which is then dried. Regular penne or maccheroni will also work with the sauce.

SERVES 4

2 aubergines, peeled, cored and diced
6 tablespoons extra virgin olive oil
2 fresh tomatoes, peeled, deseeded and diced
300g garganelli
150g ricotta cheese
4 tablespoons pecorino Romano or Parmesan cheese, plus 2 tablespoons freshly grated Parmesan cheese, to serve
20 basil leaves, torn into small pieces
Sea salt and freshly ground black pepper

1. Put the diced aubergine in a colander, sprinkle with salt and leave to stand in the sink for about 30 minutes to extract the bitter juices. Rinse and pat dry on kitchen paper.

2. Warm the oil in a frying pan and add the aubergines. Cover and fry for about 10 minutes, stirring occasionally. Add the tomatoes to the aubergines and stir to combine.

3. Bring a large saucepan of salted water to a rolling boil. Add the pasta and cook according to the package instructions until al dente (firm to the bite).

4. Meanwhile, blend the ricotta with a few tablespoons of the pasta cooking water and stir the mixture into the aubergines and tomatoes. Adjust the seasoning and remove from the heat.

5. Drain the pasta and return to the cooking saucepan. Add the aubergine, tomato and ricotta sauce, the cheese and basil. Mix together thoroughly.

6. Transfer to a warmed serving dish or individual pasta bowls and sprinkle with the remaining Parmesan just before serving.

TAGLIATELLINE SOUFFLÉ

SERVES 4

50g unsalted butter, plus extra
    for greasing
50g plain white flour
250ml milk
75g freshly grated Parmesan cheese
2 eggs, separated, plus 2 egg yolks
300g tagliatelline
Sea salt and freshly ground
    black pepper

1. Preheat the oven to 190°C/375°F/Gas Mark 5. Meanwhile, butter a 20–25-cm soufflé dish, or 4 individual dishes, and set aside.

2. Melt 50g butter in a small saucepan over a medium heat. When it foams, remove from the heat. Add the flour and stir to make a smooth paste (roux).

3. Pour in the milk, return to the heat and whisk until completely smooth. Season the sauce with salt and pepper and simmer, stirring occasionally, for 15–20 minutes.

4. Remove from the heat and cool until just warm enough to handle easily and so that it is not hot enough to cook the eggs. To prevent a skin forming on the surface, whisk through about 2 tablespoons cold water.

5. Stir in the Parmesan and then the egg yolks, one at a time. Whisk lightly during this process to incorporate as much air as possible. Set aside until needed.

6. Bring a large saucepan of salted water to the boil and add the pasta. Cook for 2–3 minutes, drain and add to the sauce. Stir gently to combine and leave to cool.

7. Whisk the egg whites until stiff peaks form and then carefully fold into the mixture. Gently pour into the soufflé dish, holding the bowl high above the dish to incorporate as much air as you can into the soufflé.

8. Place in the centre of the oven, bake for 25 minutes and then serve at once, before the soufflé collapses.

PASTA WITH FOUR CHEESES

The trick here is to get the balance of the four cheeses exactly right, so that the individual flavours shine through, rather than it tasting just like an ordinary cheese sauce. The truffle, which is an optional extra, adds luxury to an already rich and delicious sauce.

SERVES 4–6

350ml single cream
100g ripe Gorgonzola cheese
100g fontina cheese
100g Gruyère or Emmenthal cheese
100g Parmesan cheese, grated
400g conchiglie, penne, maccheroni
    or fusilli
120ml milk
2 free-range egg yolks
Shaved truffle (optional)
Sea salt and freshly ground black
    pepper

1. Pour the cream into a heatproof bowl and set over a pan of simmering water to warm through.

2. Remove the rind and dice the soft cheeses. Add all the cheeses to the cream to melt, stirring gently and frequently.

3. Meanwhile, bring a large saucepan of salted water to a rolling boil and cook the pasta until al dente (firm to the bite) according to the package directions.

4. When the cheese has melted into the cream, remove from the heat and slacken with milk to make the texture easier to distribute through the pasta. Add freshly ground black pepper to taste and mix in the egg yolks.

5. Drain the cooked pasta and return it to the cooking saucepan to retain the heat. Pour over the sauce, mix together well and transfer to a warmed serving dish. Quickly shave over the truffle, if using, and serve at once.

PENNE WITH EGGS & SAUSAGE

This deliciously rich combination of eggs and tasty sausages makes a really filling pasta dish. It's a little similar to a classic Carbonara, but here, the pancetta is substituted with the grainy texture of sausage.

SERVES 6

3 eggs, plus 3 egg yolks
4 tablespoons freshly grated
　Parmesan cheese
5 tablespoons milk
200g Italian sausage, such as salsiccia
　di maiale or Luganega
3 tablespoons extra virgin olive oil
4 tablespoons dry white wine
500g penne
Sea salt and freshly ground
　black pepper

1. In a bowl, beat the eggs and egg yolks together with the Parmesan, milk and season well with salt and pepper.

2. Skin and crumble the sausage. Heat the oil in a large, wide frying pan and add the sausage and wine. Fry together until the sausage is cooked, stirring occasionally.

3. Bring a large saucepan of salted water to a rolling boil and add the penne. Cook according to the package directions until al dente (firm to the bite). Drain and add to the pan with the sausage.

4. Mix together well, pour in the egg mixture and gently cook over a very low heat until the eggs have just scrambled.

5. Transfer to a warmed serving dish or individual pasta bowls and serve.

ORECCHIETTE WITH CHEESE & BROCCOLI

You could use a soft, slightly sour cheese, such as stracchino, instead of the young pecorino if you prefer — this will give you a creamier finished dish.

SERVES 4

300g orecchiette
2 tablespoons unsalted butter
1 shallot, peeled and finely chopped
120g broccoli florets, cooked until
   just tender
5 tablespoons extra virgin olive oil
280g freshly grated young pecorino
   cheese
Freshly grated Parmesan cheese,
   to serve
Sea salt and freshly ground
   black pepper

1. Bring a large saucepan of salted water to a rolling boil and add the orecchiette. Cook until al dente (firm to the bite) according to the package directions and then drain.

2. Heat the butter in a wide pan and fry the shallot until pale golden. Add the cooked broccoli and the oil, then stir together until heated through.

3. Season with salt and pepper to taste. Add a little of the water in which the pasta is cooking if the mixture appears to be drying out too much.

4. Drain the pasta, transfer to the pan with the broccoli and mix together well. Stir in the grated pecorino and adjust the seasoning.

5. Transfer to a warmed serving dish or individual pasta bowls. Serve at once, offering freshly grated Parmesan separately.

SPAGHETTI WITH PECORINO & BLACK PEPPER

This classic dressing for pasta calls for young, slightly soft pecorino cheese to give the dish a salty, tangy flavour, but Parmesan may be substituted instead.

SERVES 6

500g spaghetti
150g young pecorino cheese, grated
6 tablespoons extra virgin olive oil
1 tablespoon freshly ground
   black pepper
Sea salt

1. Bring a large saucepan of salted water to a rolling boil, then add the pasta and cook until al dente (firm to the bite) according to the package instructions.

2. Drain the pasta and return to the saucepan in which it was cooked.

3. Add the grated cheese to the pasta and mix together with the oil and 2–3 tablespoons of the water in which the pasta was cooked.

4. Once thoroughly mixed, add the freshly ground black pepper and transfer to a warmed serving dish or individual bowls. Serve at once.

CANNELLONI WITH VEAL & CHEESE FILLING

SERVES 6

75g unsalted butter
300g stewing veal
200g prosciutto cotto (cooked ham)
1 egg
100g freshly grated Parmesan cheese
½ litre Béchamel sauce, warmed
   (see pages 60–61)
Sea salt
PASTA
500g plain white flour, 00, plus extra
   for rolling out
5 eggs
A pinch of sea salt

1. Preheat the oven to 190°C/375°F/Gas Mark 5.

2. Make the fresh pasta (see pages 19–20). Roll out on a floured surface as thinly as possible, then cut into rectangles about the size of your hand.

3. Bring a pan of salted water to a rolling boil, then cook the pasta sheets in batches, 3 sheets at a time. As soon as the sheets rise to the surface, remove with a slotted spoon and lay flat in a wide bowl or tray of cold water to prevent them sticking together.

4. Heat about one-third of the butter in a large frying pan and quickly fry the veal until well browned.

5. Mince or process finely with the ham. Stir in the egg and the cheese, and then season with salt.

6. Divide the veal filling between the drained pasta sheets and roll up to form the cannelloni. Generously butter an ovenproof dish and arrange the rolls inside, side by side.

7. Cover the pasta rolls with Béchamel sauce, dot with any remaining butter and heat through in the oven until golden and bubbling hot, about 5–10 minutes. Serve at once.

PASTA TIP
This recipe is also delicious made with pancakes instead of the pasta sheets. You will require 6 pancakes made in a 10-cm frying pan.

PAPPARDELLE WITH GRANA PADANO

Grana Padano cheese is very similar to Parmigiano Reggiano, but comes from Lombardy instead of Emilia Romagna. Both cheeses can be used in precisely the same ways and are interchangeable.

SERVES 6

4 tablespoons extra virgin olive oil, plus extra for drizzling
4 garlic cloves, peeled and finely chopped
4 plump spring onions, finely chopped (discard the hard green tops)
1 dry bay leaf
3 thick-cut pancetta or streaky bacon rashers, roughly chopped
300g pappardelle
200g Grana Padano cheese, thinly shaved
Sea salt and freshly ground black pepper

1. Heat the olive oil in a large wide pan and fry together the garlic, spring onions, bay leaf and pancetta or bacon until the onions are soft and the pancetta or bacon is crispy.

2. Meanwhile, bring a large saucepan of salted water to a rolling boil, then add the pappardelle and cook until al dente (firm to the bite) according to the package directions.

3. Drain and return the pasta to the pan with the other ingredients. Add half the shaved Grana Padano and salt and pepper to taste, and toss together well.

4. Place the dressed pappardelle in the centre of a warmed serving platter and cover with the remaining cheese. Finally drizzle with oil just before serving.

FUSILLI WITH SCAMORZA & MUSHROOMS

Scamorza is an aged mozzarella and available smoked or unsmoked. The soaking liquid from the porcini is usually very bitter, so taste before you decide to keep it for a soup or stew!

SERVES 4

60g dried porcini mushrooms (see tip)
5 tablespoons unsalted butter
$\frac{1}{2}$ glass of dry white wine
400g fusilli
200g smoked scamorza, grated
5 tablespoons freshly grated Parmesan cheese
Sea salt and freshly ground black pepper

1. Rinse the dried mushrooms, then leave to soak in enough hot water to cover for about 20 minutes, or until softened.

2. Meanwhile, bring a large saucepan of salted water to a rolling boil.

3. Drain and coarsely chop the mushrooms. Heat half the butter in a frying pan. Add the chopped mushrooms and the wine and gently cook together for about 10 minutes.

4. Add the fusilli to the boiling water and cook until al dente (firm to the bite) according to the package directions. Drain and return to the warm cooking saucepan.

5. Add the mushrooms, grated scamorza, half the Parmesan and plenty of freshly ground black pepper to the pasta and mix together thoroughly.

6. Transfer to a warmed serving dish or into individual pasta bowls. Sprinkle with the rest of the Parmesan and serve at once.

PASTA TIP

When using dried porcini, soak them for plenty of time before use so they are really soft. Carefully remove from the soaking liquid to avoid adding any grit that may have been on the mushrooms to the sauce.

PENNE WITH CARAMELIZED RED ONIONS

This pasta dish makes the most of the freshest ricotta available in the springtime and also the intensely sweet flavour of fat and juicy, purplish onions.

SERVES 4

4 tablespoons extra virgin olive oil
2 large red onions, peeled and finely sliced
400g penne
5 tablespoons fresh ricotta cheese
6 smoked streaky bacon or pancetta rashers, grilled and chopped
3 tablespoons freshly grated Parmesan cheese, to serve
2 tablespoons chopped flat leaf parsley, to garnish
Sea salt and freshly ground black pepper

1. Bring a large saucepan of salted water to a rolling boil.

2. Meanwhile, heat the oil and fry the onions very slowly, stirring frequently, until the onions are dense, soft and sweet, then season with salt and pepper.

3. Boil the pasta until al dente (firm to the bite) according to the package directions. Drain well and return to the saucepan in which it was cooked.

4. Pour over the onions and add the ricotta and bacon. Mix thoroughly.

5. Transfer to a warmed serving dish or individual plates. Sprinkle with Parmesan and chopped parsley, then serve at once.

PENNE WITH SOFT GOATS' CHEESE

This is a very simple recipe that is fresh and delicious, with lots of different flavours including the sweetness of the tomatoes, the salty capers and the slightly sour tang of the goats' cheese.

SERVES 4

5 tablespoons extra virgin olive oil
1 garlic clove, peeled and lightly crushed
500g fresh ripe tomatoes, skinned and coarsely chopped
1 dessertspoon salted capers, rinsed, dried and coarsely chopped
15 green olives, pitted
225g soft, creamy goats' cheese
350g penne
1 small handful of basil leaves, torn into pieces
Sea salt and freshly ground black pepper

1. Bring a large saucepan of salted water to a rolling boil.
2. Meanwhile, heat the oil and garlic together until the garlic is pungent and golden, then discard the garlic and add the tomatoes.
3. Mix together and cook for about 5 minutes, then stir in the capers and olives. Cook for a further 5 minutes, season and take off the heat. Keep warm.
4. Mash the goats' cheese with 2–3 tablespoons of the pasta cooking water and season with pepper.
5. Cook the pasta until al dente (firm to the bite) according to the package directions. Drain and return to the warm cooking saucepan.
6. Add the tomato sauce, goats' cheese and basil to the pasta. Mix together thoroughly and serve at once on a warmed serving dish or in individual pasta bowls.

PIPETTE WITH EGG & CHEESE

You can use any shape pasta for this very comforting dish, but pipette (short, narrow maccheroni) will work well. For a little touch of luxury, add a little cream to the egg yolks just before stirring through.

SERVES 4

400g ribbed pipette
55g unsalted butter
3 egg yolks, beaten
6 tablespoons freshly grated
   Parmesan cheese
1 small handful of flat leaf parsley,
   rinsed and dried, then finely
   chopped (see tip), to garnish
Sea salt and freshly ground
   black pepper

1. Bring a large saucepan of salted water to a rolling boil, then add the pipette. Stir once and cook until al dente (firm to the bite) according to the package directions.

2. Drain the pasta and return it to the saucepan in which it was cooked. Add the butter and mix together thoroughly.

3. Stir in the egg yolks and Parmesan, then transfer to a warmed serving dish or pasta bowls. Serve at once, sprinkled with chopped parsley and freshly ground black pepper.

PASTA TIP
Before chopping the parsley stalks, remove the leaves and discard any tough stalks. To vary the flavour, you could add other herbs such as basil or fresh thyme.

ZITI WITH GORGONZOLA

One of the oldest pasta shapes, ziti is also one of the first ever produced on an industrial level. It resembles longer than usual maccheroni, but any short, tubular shape will also work with this delicious, creamy sauce.

SERVES 4

400g ziti
225g Gorgonzola cheese, rind
   removed and diced
5 tablespoons milk
2 tablespoons double cream
1 handful of flat leaf parsley, chopped
Sea salt and freshly ground
   black pepper

1. Bring a large saucepan of salted water to a rolling boil. Add the ziti and cook until al dente (firm to the bite) according to the package instructions.
2. Meanwhile, put the diced Gorgonzola in a large frying pan with the milk and cream. Gently heat through to melt the cheese, stirring frequently.
3. Stir the parsley into the Gorgonzola sauce and season with a little freshly ground black pepper.
4. Drain the pasta and tip it into the pan with the sauce. Mix together well and then transfer to a warmed serving platter or pasta bowls to serve at once.

STUFFED CONCHIGLIE

In Italian, *conchiglie* means seashells – which is exactly what the shape of this pasta resembles. Fill with ricotta before dressing them to transform the shells into a very special dish, especially if you use the larger variety of this popular shape.

SERVES 4

300g large conchiglie
4 tablespoons extra virgin olive oil
200g fresh ricotta cheese
250g chopped pancetta
4 ripe tomatoes, roughly chopped
100g fresh peas
75g grated pecorino or Parmesan
   cheese, to serve
1 tablespoon finely chopped flat leaf
   parsley, to garnish
Sea salt and freshly ground
   black pepper

1. Preheat the oven to 170°C/325°F/Gas Mark 3.

2. Meanwhile, bring a large saucepan of salted water to a rolling boil. Add the conchiglie and cook until al dente (firm to the bite) according to the package directions.

3. Drain and refresh the pasta under cold running water. Drain once more and oil very lightly, then set aside until needed.

4. In a bowl, mix together the ricotta with seasoning to taste. Using a piping bag fitted with a small nozzle or a teaspoon, fill the conchiglie with the cheese.

5. Heat three-quarters of the oil in a wide frying pan and fry the pancetta until crisp. Stir in the tomatoes and peas, and then cook together for about 10 minutes, stirring frequently. Season to taste.

6. Add the filled conchiglie and mix together gently over a medium heat. Transfer to an ovenproof dish, loosely cover with foil and heat through thoroughly, about 10 minutes.

7. Remove the dish from the oven and sprinkle with pecorino or Parmesan. Drizzle over the remaining oil and add a little freshly ground black pepper. Finally, sprinkle with parsley and serve at once.

PENNE WITH RICOTTA & GORGONZOLA

Gorgonzola is the famous blue cheese from the Lombard town of the same name and can be bought in two versions: sweet or piquant. Although this recipe suggests using the sweet variety, feel free to use the more intensely flavoured piquant cheese, if you prefer.

SERVES 6

300g fresh ricotta cheese
100g sweet Gorgonzola cheese
500g penne
Sea salt and freshly ground
   black pepper

1. Place the ricotta in a large bowl and mash with a fork. Add the Gorgonzola and some freshly ground black pepper and continue to blend together.

2. Meanwhile, bring a large saucepan of salted water to a rolling boil and use a little of the boiling water to slake the ricotta mixture until smooth.

3. Add the penne to the water and cook until al dente (firm to the bite) according to the package directions. Drain and transfer to the bowl containing the ricotta mixture.

4. Mix the penne and the ricotta together well (if necessary, add a little more of the pasta cooking water to help distribute the ricotta through the pasta). Transfer to a warmed serving dish and serve at once.

RIGATONI WITH RICOTTA, PARSLEY & BASIL

Rigatoni are large, ridged maccheroni. This is a simple sauce that requires no cooking. In the absence of a food processor, chop the herbs very finely and mix into the ricotta.

SERVES 4

180g fresh ricotta cheese
3 tablespoons finely chopped flat leaf parsley, plus extra to serve
1 small handful of basil leaves, torn into small shreds
5 tablespoons double cream
350g rigatoni
5 tablespoons freshly grated Parmesan cheese
Sea salt and freshly ground black pepper

1. Bring a large saucepan of salted water to a rolling boil.

2. Meanwhile, whizz together the ricotta, parsley and basil in a food processor. Season the resulting sauce with salt and pepper, transfer to a bowl and stir in the cream.

3. Add the rigatoni to the boiling water and cook until al dente (firm to the bite) according to the package directions. Drain and return to the saucepan in which it was cooked.

4. Add the sauce and half the Parmesan to the pasta; mix together well. Transfer to a warmed serving dish or pasta bowls and sprinkle with the remaining cheese and extra parsley just before serving.

SPAGHETTI ALLA CAPRICCIOSA

This is the true taste of an Italian summer, with all those wonderfully fresh flavours, tempered by the fresh creaminess of mozzarella. It's one of the easiest, yet most delicious of all the sauces.

SERVES 6

10 tablespoons extra virgin olive oil
500g fresh tomatoes, peeled,
   deseeded and coarsely chopped
8 basil leaves, torn into shreds
1 dessertspoon dried oregano
6 tablespoons freshly grated
   Parmesan cheese
500g spaghetti
300g fresh Buffalo mozzarella cheese
Sea salt and freshly ground
   black pepper

1. Mix the oil with the tomatoes in a bowl, then stir in the basil, oregano and grated Parmesan. Leave to stand for a couple of hours, or chill overnight in the refrigerator if possible.

2. When you are ready to serve, bring a large saucepan of salted water to a rolling boil and cook the spaghetti until al dente (firm to the bite) according to the package directions.

3. Meanwhile, cut the mozzarella into small pieces and place in the bottom of a large serving bowl.

4. Drain the spaghetti and pour it over the mozzarella. Mix together quickly, adding the tomato sauce. Adjust the seasoning and serve at once.

PASTA TIP

If you decide to chill the tomato sauce, remember to bring it back to room temperature before using otherwise it will cool the pasta down too quickly. You could also make this recipe into a pasta salad: use short pasta that has been cooled in cold water after cooking and dress with the chilled sauce.

GNOCCHETTI SARDI WITH RICOTTA

Also known as *malloreddus*, gnocchetti Sardi are the traditional pasta of the island of Sardinia. They look like small, elongated conch shells and are deliciously firm and chewy.

SERVES 4

400g gnocchetti Sardi
3 tablespoons extra virgin olive oil
1 small onion, peeled and chopped
1 small handful of flat leaf parsley,
   rinsed and chopped
400g canned tomatoes
150g fresh ricotta cheese
Sea salt and freshly ground
   black pepper

1. Bring a large saucepan of salted water to a rolling boil and cook the pasta until al dente (firm to the bite) according to the package directions.

2. Meanwhile, heat the oil and fry the onion and parsley together until the onion has softened. Stir in the canned tomatoes and leave to simmer for about 10 minutes.

3. Add the ricotta and mix together thoroughly until you have achieved a lovely dense, creamy texture, then transfer the sauce to a deep bowl.

4. Drain the pasta and pile it on top of the sauce. Toss together well, season with freshly ground black pepper and serve at once.

DISCHI VOLANTI WITH RICOTTA & PINE KERNELS

The choice of dischi volanti (flying saucer shaped pasta) for this dish is purely personal, but I do think that a flat, rounded shape does work rather well with this sauce. Ruote (wheels) make a good alternative.

SERVES 4

300g dischi volanti or similar pasta shape
6 tablespoons extra virgin olive oil
1 garlic clove, peeled and lightly crushed
2 tablespoons pine kernels
2 tablespoons shelled chopped walnuts
120g fresh ricotta cheese
6 basil leaves, bruised and torn into pieces, plus extra to garnish
1 handful of parsley, finely chopped
2–3 tablespoons freshly grated Parmesan cheese, to serve
Sea salt and freshly ground black pepper

1. Bring a large saucepan of salted water to a rolling boil. Add the pasta and cook according to the package directions until al dente (firm to the bite).

2. Meanwhile, heat the olive oil in a pan and gently fry the crushed garlic with the pine kernels until the garlic is pungent and the pine kernels turn a golden brown.

3. Take the pan off the heat, discard the garlic and add the walnuts. Mix together briefly, then stir in the ricotta and herbs, adding a little of the pasta cooking water to help blend everything together.

4. Drain the pasta and return it to the saucepan in which it was cooked. Add the ricotta mixture and toss together to distribute the sauce evenly.

5. Transfer to a warmed serving dish or individual pasta bowls and serve sprinkled with Parmesan and freshly ground black pepper, and garnished with extra basil leaves.

SPELT FUSILLI WITH SAFFRON & CREAM

Dried pasta is not only available as durum wheat pasta but can also be made from other grains, such as spelt or a combination of barley or millet and others – good news for those with a wheat intolerance.

SERVES 4

350g spelt fusilli
6 tablespoons extra virgin olive oil
15g powdered saffron
2 large handfuls of basil leaves, rinsed
  and torn into shreds
3 tablespoons single cream
4–5 tablespoons freshly grated
  pecorino cheese
Sea salt and freshly ground
  black pepper

1. Bring a large saucepan of salted water to a rolling boil. Add the fusilli and cook until al dente (firm to the bite) according to the package instructions.

2. Meanwhile, warm the olive oil with the saffron and basil for about 10 minutes, then season with salt and pepper.

3. Drain the fusilli and return it to the cooking saucepan. Pour over the infused oil and cream and then mix together well until both are distributed through the pasta.

4. Add half the pecorino and mix again.

5. Transfer to a warmed serving dish or individual bowls. Sprinkle with the remaining pecorino and serve at once.

PASTA WITH LEMON & CREAM SAUCE

This is a light and simple pasta dish that really makes the most of those lemons that have overwintered and in the spring are bursting with intense flavour.

SERVES 4

400g penne, ruote or conchiglie
40g unsalted butter
Grated zest of 2 large lemons
Juice of 1 lemon
½ glass of dry white wine
10 tablespoons single cream or
    crème fraîche
2–3 tablespoons finely chopped
    flat leaf parsley or basil
4 tablespoons freshly grated
    Parmesan cheese
Sea salt and freshly ground
    black pepper

1. Bring a large saucepan of salted water to a rolling boil, then add the pasta and cook until al dente (firm to the bite) according to the package directions.

2. Meanwhile, melt the butter in a large, wide frying pan and add the lemon zest. Gently fry for about 5 minutes.

3. Add the lemon juice to the butter and lemon zest, then stir in the white wine and boil rapidly for about 2 minutes. Add the cream or crème fraîche and black pepper, stirring.

4. Drain the pasta well and then add to the frying pan. Stir together to thoroughly coat the pasta. Add the parsley or basil and half the Parmesan; mix together once more.

5. Remove from the heat and transfer to a warmed platter or individual plates. Sprinkle with the remaining cheese and serve at once.

RAVIOLI WITH BEETROOT & MASCARPONE FILLING

SERVES 4

2 large beetroot, boiled for
   10–15 minutes
6 tablespoons mascarpone cheese
2 tablespoons freshly grated
   Parmesan cheese, plus extra
   to serve
A large pinch of ground cumin
Sea salt and freshly ground black
   pepper
PASTA
400g plain white pasta flour, 00,
   plus extra for rolling out
4 large eggs
DRESSING
100g unsalted butter
1½ teaspoons poppy seeds

PASTA TIP
*Spoon any leftover filling
over freshly boiled pasta
as a dressing.*

1. Carefully drain the beetroot and leave to cool until just warm, but not cold. Peel and dice, then process or liquidize until completely smooth.

2. Add the mascarpone to make a smooth, thick purée. Stir in the Parmesan and ground cumin, then season to taste. Chill until required.

3. To make the ravioli, make the fresh pasta as usual (see pages 19–20), then roll the dough out as thinly as possible on a floured surface. Fold it in half and roll out again. Repeat 6 times. (If using a pasta machine, roll it out to the penultimate thickness.) Trim to 8 sheets, each one about 24 x 10cm.

4. Drop 4 tablespoons of filling along 4 of the sheets, leaving a border all the way round. Top with the other 4 sheets; cut into 4 across the width and then cut around the edges, away from the filling with a pastry wheel to make 16 ravioli (4 per sheet). Be sure to seal the edges well with your fingertips, or a little water if the pasta starts to dry out.

5. Melt the butter until liquid and nutty, but not dark brown. Stir in the poppy seeds and leave to infuse for about 15 minutes.

6. Meanwhile, bring a large saucepan of salted water (or light vegetable stock) to a rolling boil. Slide in the ravioli and boil just until they float on the surface and the pasta is tender, about 4–5 minutes. Remove and divide between warmed serving plates.

7. Drizzle poppy seed butter over each portion of ravioli and serve at once, with freshly grated Parmesan offered separately.

ORECCHIETTE PASTA SALAD WITH MOZZARELLA

This is a classic pasta salad recipe from southern Italy that celebrates many of the ingredients typifying the cuisine of the area.

SERVES 6

600g cherry tomatoes, rinsed and
   sliced in half
300g Buffalo mozzarella, diced
1 handful of capers preserved in oil,
   drained
1 tablespoon dried oregano
1 small handful of basil leaves,
   rinsed, dried and torn into shreds
1 garlic clove, peeled and very finely
   chopped
8 tablespoons extra virgin olive oil
500g orecchiette
Sea salt and freshly ground
   black pepper

1. In the bowl that you plan to use for serving the pasta, place the tomatoes, mozzarella, capers, oregano, basil, garlic and oil. Mix together well and leave to stand for about 30 minutes to allow the flavours to infuse.

2. Meanwhile, bring a large saucepan of salted water to a rolling boil. Add the orecchiette and cook until al dente (firm to the bite) according to the package directions.

3. Refresh the pasta under cold running water, drain and tip into the serving bowl with the other salad ingredients. Mix together well, adjust the seasoning to taste and serve at once.

BAVETTE WITH ZESTY LEMON SAUCE

A very tangy, extremely light pasta dish, dressed with a sauce that requires no cooking at all. Use a combination of lemon and lime if you prefer, or even orange zest for a sweeter taste.

SERVES 6

400g bavette
8 tablespoons fresh ricotta cheese
3 tablespoons milk
2 tablespoons grated lemon zest
3 tablespoons finely chopped parsley
4 tablespoons freshly grated
   Parmesan cheese, to serve
Sea salt and freshly ground
   black pepper

1. Bring a large saucepan of salted water to a rolling boil. Add the pasta and stir well.

2. Cover with a lid and return to the boil. Remove the lid and boil the pasta, uncovered, until al dente (firm to the bite) according to the package directions.

3. Meanwhile, mash the ricotta cheese with the milk to make it creamy. Stir in the lemon zest and parsley; season with a little salt and pepper.

4. Drain the pasta and return it to the cooking saucepan. Pour over the sauce and toss together well. Transfer to a warmed serving dish, sprinkle with the Parmesan cheese and serve at once.

FILLED PASTA ROLL WITH CHEESE & WALNUTS

The trick with this recipe is to master the art of making a wide, fine and smooth square of pasta. Once this has been achieved, you can vary the filling according to preference.

SERVES 6–8

400g fresh ricotta cheese
200g mascarpone cheese
5 tablespoons shelled walnuts,
    coarsely chopped
2 eggs, beaten
5 tablespoons freshly grated
    Parmesan cheese, plus extra
    to serve
A pinch of grated nutmeg or mace
Sea salt and freshly ground
    black pepper
PASTA
500g plain white pasta flour, 00,
    plus extra for rolling out
5 eggs
TOMATO SAUCE
4 tablespoons olive oil
2–3 garlic cloves, crushed
400g canned tomatoes, deseeded and
    coarsely chopped

1. Mix the ricotta and mascarpone to make a reasonably even, smooth textured filling. Stir in the walnuts, ensuring they are evenly distributed.

2. In another bowl, mix together the eggs and Parmesan, then blend into the cheese and walnut filling. Finally, season with nutmeg, salt and pepper – the filling will now have a spreading consistency. (Note: don't be tempted to combine with a food processor – the resulting mixture will be too fine.)

3. To make the pasta dough, tip the flour out onto a work surface. Make a well in the centre with your closed fist and then break the eggs inside.

4. Begin to stir the eggs into the flour using the fingertips of one hand or a fork. Use the other hand to help you push the flour into the centre as you stir.

5. When the eggs are incorporated into the flour, use both hands to knead the mixture together into a ball of dough (see pasta tip on page 178). Cover and rest for about 20 minutes.

6. On a floured surface, roll the dough out into a large, wide, long sheet as thinly as possible. If using a pasta machine, wind the pasta through the

1 bay leaf

A pinch of dried marjoram

Sea salt and freshly ground
   black pepper

rollers to the penultimate setting on the machine. As the roll cannot be bent, make sure your saucepan is wide enough to allow it to lie straight in the water; do not make the roll longer than the width of the saucepan.

7. Spread the filling evenly over the surface to within 4cm of the edges. Roll up like a Swiss roll and then lay the roll on a sheet of clean muslin or a large napkin.

8. Roll the cloth around the roll and tie the ends together securely. Leave the ends fairly long so that you can transport the roll more easily.

9. Bring a large deep and wide saucepan of salted water to a rolling boil and then carefully lower the roll into it. Boil gently for 35–45 minutes, depending on the thickness of the roll. Do not let it sag in the centre!

10. Meanwhile, make the sauce: heat the olive oil and gently fry the garlic for about 8 minutes until golden. Stir in the tomatoes.

11. Add the bay leaf, marjoram and seasoning. Cover and simmer gently for about 15 minutes. Remove the lid and increase the heat slightly for a further 15 minutes. Remove the bay leaf and keep warm.

12. Carefully remove the pasta roll from the water and lay on a chopping board. Unwrap the cloth, then slice the roll into rounds and arrange them on a warmed platter.

13. Drizzle with the sauce, or serve the sauce separately in a sauceboat. Serve hot, with freshly grated Parmesan.

PASTA TIP

Once you have made a ball of dough, roll it out and fold it in half, then roll it out again. Continue in this way until a shiny, cool, elastic sheet of dough is achieved, or put the dough into the food processor. Using the blade attachment, whizz for about 45 seconds. Both methods ensure the dough will be smooth and can easily be rolled out.

CONCHIGLIE WITH AVOCADO & RICOTTA SAUCE

This pasta dish is dressed with a lovely pale green sauce, which requires no cooking at all and is ideal for hot summer days. The shape of the conchiglie holds the sauce perfectly.

SERVES 6

400g conchiglie
2 avocados, peeled and mashed
7 tablespoons fresh ricotta cheese
2 tablespoons milk or single cream
1 tablespoon chopped parsley or
   coriander
Sea salt and freshly ground
   black pepper
TO SERVE
Freshly grated Parmesan cheese
Extra avocado, diced and sliced
   (optional)

1. Bring a large saucepan of salted water to a rolling boil. Add the pasta, stir well and then cover and boil until al dente (firm to the bite) according to the package directions.

2. Meanwhile, beat the mashed avocado with the ricotta and milk or cream to make a fairly smooth sauce. Season the mixture with salt, then stir in the parsley or coriander. Finally, season with plenty of black pepper.

3. Drain the pasta and return to the saucepan. Add the green sauce and toss together well to coat. Transfer to a warmed serving bowl and serve at once, with freshly grated Parmesan and avocado slices and cubes, if liked.

INDEX